Sword
of
No
Blade

JOAN BAXTER

SAMUEL WEISER, INC.

York Beach, Maine

First published in 1992 by
Samuel Weiser, Inc.
Box 612
York Beach, Maine 03910

Library of Congress Cataloging-in-Publication Data

Baxter, Joan, 1935–
    Sword of no blade / by Joan Baxter.
      p.   cm.
    1. Karate. 2. Yoga. I. Title
    GV1114.3.B39 1992
    796.8'153—dc20   92-1773
                                         CIP

ISBN 0-87728-748-1
CCP

Illustrations, pages 6, 18, 20, 24, 28, 34, 40, 46, 50, 52, 54,
56, 60, 62, 66, 76, 84, 106, 114, 120, 139 Copyright © 1992
Terry Dukes
Illustrations, pages xx, 30, 72, 80, 88, 96, 105, 112, 128, 130,
134 Copyright © 1992 Joan Baxter

Cover art copyright © 1992 Terry Dukes
Used by kind permission.

Printed in the United States of America

The paper used in this publication meets the minimum re-
quirements of the American National Standard for Perma-
nence of Paper for Printed Library Materials Z39.48-1984.

Dedicated to my
late father
and
the memory of
O. H. Searle

India	China	Japan
Dhyana	Cha'an	Zen

Zen is not a religion
Zen is not a myth
Zen is not
Zen is
Zen
!

Contents

Preface

My introduction to karate was not caused by the two years I spent in Hong Kong and the New Territories, although the soft, flowing movements that I saw being practiced in the early morning in every green space fascinated me. My host from Shanghai told me that it was called "Chinese Boxing." I had not heard of the art of Tai Chi at that time. Nor was my introduction to karate to come during the year I spent traveling around Japan and the Ryuku Islands. Strangely, I had to return from the East to the West, after ten years of travel, to be fired with an Eastern art.

Indirectly my introduction to karate was through yoga. Yoga was something I had become interested in through various encounters during my travels. In particular, one yogi I met in the lower Himalayas, not far from Chober (one of the cave dwellings of Tibet's great yogi Milarepa), was my first introduction to physical Yoga. His name was Cancha, and unlike most yogis, mendicants, or *sanyasen* (renunciants), he was not simply contemplative, nor did he practice a life of austerity.

Cancha slipped from one yoga posture to the next with oiled ease. Yet afterwards, he told me through an interpreter that of the eighty-four basic postures—which legend says, Lord Shiva, the Destroyer, performed with a thousand variations on each—he could do only eighty-two. I was puzzled. How could one so adept, so dedicated, be stuck at the last two poses? Could they really be so difficult, or demanding? What was holding him back?

Cancha's answer was practical: "If I do the last two postures, I am full yogi. Full yogi does not eat meat or eggs, and I *like* meat and eggs." Perhaps Cancha was a Zen Master, too. Final, as well as first steps, seem to have their own unique pressures.

Once during my travels, a Hindu couple who had never seen me before, greeted me with "Your food is waiting for you. It only remains for you to come and eat it." I accompanied them to their home on the lower slopes of the Himalayas. We talked like old friends, and I found them stimulating and philosophical. In one room of their home, they ran a school called the Vydhia Mundha (the Temple of Wisdom). They told me of their friend, Sobha Singh, an artist, recluse, and spiritual teacher who, it seemed, had a difficulty with last steps similar to Cancha.

Sobha Singh normally did not receive visitors, but my hosts felt that if I went with them, he would see me. He was a *bodhisattva*, the couple told me, one who stops short of *nirvana* (enlightenment) to stay on this worldly plane of existence to help others.

One day's journey away, in a simple garden amid mountain grandeur and fast-flowing icy water, Sobha Singh and I met. Despite my preparation, I felt overwhelmed. His portraits of the people who had sat for him, including Mahatma Gandhi and the Rani of Kashmir, were utterly lifelike. I almost expected them to speak. His scenes of people and nature lured me to walk into them. The light his paintings radiated came from a depth that surely reflected the man's inner self. Yet when I asked him how he achieved this effect, he said that it was just the opposite of putting himself in the paintings.

"Meditation. Give yourself up entirely to the sitter. Become one. Annihilate self, so that nothing of the artist goes into the painting, so that he paints not as he sees, or wants to see, but as the person or place *is*."

Over a simple vegetarian meal, eaten by candlelight, he told me of his time as a sannyasi, living off the land, in solitude, in the wild. Through meditating and fasting, he lost all sense of time. Then he reached the point when he had become so detached from the world that he had to decide—decide before the point of no return. Beyond that point, he would never paint again. He battled with himself. Should he take what he had been seeking, now that it was so close? Or, should he go back?

Fortunately, he decided to stay in this realm, to paint, and to help others spiritually. "But," he admitted, "I still wonder sometimes: where would I be now had I not come back—had I gone on?" Like Cancha, his path was best expressed in active rather than passive meditation.

Between the Himalayas, with their ancient secret wisdom, and the Hindu Kush, with its rugged beauty, lie the impressive peaks of the Karakorams. From here, I went south over the Babusar Pass, going from desert heat up to icy winter, and down again into the beautiful Kaghan Valley. Here, I met two fire-worshippers. One of these Zoroastrians, Soli, a gentle, spiritual man, explained that they got their name—fire-worshippers—because they worshipped the everlasting fire that burns within. Though frugal with himself, fasting often, he was generous to others. His friend, Jehangir, attacked the mountains and life with vigor. Both were vegetarian—Jehangir, because he thought it healthier for himself, and Soli, because he thought it healthier for the animals.

When Soli suggested I seek an audience with His Holiness, the Dalai Lama of Tibet, I felt stunned. Who was I to waste such a great man's time? He must have enough on his mind, I thought, considering the plight of his country and his people. Soli pressed the issue, saying that his friend, Phiroz Mehta, author of many spiritual works, had been granted such an audience and that he had greatly benefitted. Soli felt sure I would benefit also. I was sure I would, too, but I was hesitant.

I traveled with them for two days more, amid tall firs, great rocks, and snow-laden mountains. At the foot of Malika Purbat, melting ice darted beneath snow bridges and through tunnels on its way down to the lake. When the time came for us to part, I was still sure I would not seek an audience with the Dalai Lama, despite Soli's quiet persistence. However, I did promise Soli that I would at least visit Dharamsala, the home of His Holiness in exile in the Himalayan foothills of India.

About a year later, in 1963, I reached Dharamsala, four years after His Holiness's escape to India where he could continue to give hope to his people. I found them to be immensely lovable and loving people possessing a quality I had never known. No matter what the circumstances, I never met a bitter Tibetan. Ultimately, the Tibetan people themselves decided for me, and I wrote that letter requesting an audience with His Holiness. I felt excited and nervous when a letter arrived bearing the seal of the Tibetan Government—an audience had been granted.

I was even more nervous when the special day itself arrived. As I ascended to McLeod Ganj, a deadening blanket of white lay over the countryside. A gray sky wafted low, swirling mistily through the slim trees. Soon, I reached Swargashram, the residence of His Holiness, where two guards stamped in the snow and blew on their numbed fingers. For a peaceful man surrounded by a community of devotees, guards seemed ludicrous to me. Mr. Sonam from Sikkim, the interpreter to His Holiness, explained that attempts from across the border were still made on the Dalai Lama's life.

Afraid that I might slip up on something important, I asked Mr. Sonam if there were any customs I should observe. "Nothing," he said, "unless you are thinking of asking His Holiness any offensive questions." I looked questioningly. Mr. Sonam continued shyly, "Like asking His Holiness if he is a god." Such a question had not entered my head. All the same, when I heard the words "His Holiness is ready now," I felt anything but ready.

I walked up the steps of the bungalow and found myself facing a smiling figure. I brought my hands together in greeting and was surprised when His Holiness came towards me, touching my hand between both of his—almost a Western handshake. Later I was sorry that, through ignorance, I had not greeted him according to Tibetan custom, by placing a *kutah* (a white, gauzy scarf) around his neck, which is returned at the end of the audience as a precious blessing and remembrance.

We sat cross-legged on the floor and a honey-colored dog bounded in, its tail wagging, and snuggled its nose into my arm. With patience, enthusiasm, and youthful zest, His Holiness talked about motive, action and its outcome, and a feast of good things spiritual which he called the "banquetting table of Buddhism." At the head was love, compassion, and losing ourselves in thought for others—words you might expect from any spiritual person, and particularly from one who is an incarnation of Avolokitas-vara, bhodisattva of compassion. But these were not empty words from a cloistered life. Here was one who had seen a one-sided war against his people, had been forced to flee his country and those he loved, to see the destruction of everything meaningful—one who lived in the world and knew its atrocities, yet still held peace in his heart. He had no hint of bitterness. He was surely the heart of the Tibetan people, a heart that would not let them die, though so many were killed. He was a man who had, and was, living what he preached.

On the Buddhist concept of god, he picked up a wooden object to illustrate the initial atom and lifeforce of everything. Buddhism was unfolding for me as scientific in its spiritual essence and knowledge—a quiet, peaceful, practical force, rooted in life.

But it was not his words alone; it was his presence. Energy, warmth, alert twinkling eyes and the expression of amusement that frequently curled his lips—he was a man brimming with life.

When the audience was over I came away "full." Seeing my deep interest, Mr. Sonam offered me a return visit. Two days later, I was back. Drawing diagrams and using the Tibetan Wheel of Life, Mr. Sonam spoke of many things: the cave monasteries of Tibet, old Buddhist records discovered there, meditation, changing states of consciousness and the sacred lakes that, before the Chinese invasion of Tibet, had played such a large part in the seeking and finding of the next Dalai Lama (Ocean of Wisdom). By those trained with dedication in the art, the lakes can be looked into and read. When the present Dalai Lama was only two years old, the home where he lived with his parents was first seen in the lakes by the spiritual elders. Along with other images, this told them what to look for and in which direction they would find the fourteenth Dalai Lama.

Mr. Sonam had seen the lakes himself and looked into them. One lama at the Ashram, as a means of seeing and reading a surface, was practicing with red dye on his thumb. The lakes are traditional and by association have greater meaning. I have since wondered if that same knowledge outside of Tibet, frozen till needed, could be invoked through a more accessible instrument, or perhaps that far into the future the Tibetan people will have their land and lakes back again. Tibetans live wholly in the present not the past, and do not pine or whine at change.

I had spoken to His Holiness through an interpreter, but these days, he speaks directly to the world through television and other media. One day perhaps the world will be ready to listen and to respond.

From Dharamsala, I continued farther into the Himalayas, to Nepal where I saw and heard the most beautiful sight and sound I have experienced in any temple or monastery: Tibetan monks in plum-colored robes intoning mantra, as part of their religious practice, interspersed with cymbal clashing and tea drinking.

In front of each seated figure stood a silver and wooden *gompa* (monastery) tea cup. The cups are kept constantly filled with tea made in a long, wooden cylinder, where it is mixed together with butter and salt, shaken, and beaten with a wooden plunger.

The monks chant in a unique low-toned resonant pitch that tumbles forth from the depths of their being, ringing and vibrating throughout the monastery. It was like no sound or timber I had ever heard before, for Tibetan monks have the unique ability to chant in chords rather than the usual single notes, a rare accomplishment born of dedicated practice of a particular breathing technique.

In the ancient setting, with the constant replenishing of tea cups, the rich sounds of the cymbals and chords trembled through me and flowed on into every shadowy niche of stonework, thousands of years old—a living history.

I did not know it at the time, but I was traversing the region of Asia that Bodhidharma (see Introduction) must have trod on his journey north from India to China. Quietly, though, a seed was being sown that was nurtured by the many teachers I met throughout Asia, until it began to sprout. When I reached England I would seek out a yoga teacher, and I prepared myself for a long hard search.

Around Christmas of 1969, I finally arrived in England, but instead of the difficult search I had been expecting, I was surprised to find that during my ten years absence, yoga had become popular in the west and teachers were everywhere. Eagerly I asked one practicing group what kind of yoga was being offered. Expecting the reply of possibly Hatha or Raj yoga, I was puzzled to be told "council yoga." Council yoga was not something I was familiar with. Neither had I anticipated only two hours practice once a week. But, I went along—to discover that the yoga was indeed Hatha and the council part simply meant that the course was run by the local authority (called a council in England). In more ways than one, though, it proved to be a good start.

After just a few weeks, my yoga teacher told me of a seven-day residential course. A whole week of yoga! Living and studying with a teacher was what I had expected in the first place. I leapt at the chance.

However, I arrived to find myself not on a yoga course, but on an advanced karate course! Having set off that morning with the idea of being away for a week, it seemed a bit lame to go home again because of a misunderstanding. So I stayed. When someone asked if I had a *gi*, I didn't know where to look first. So someone lent me what turned out to be the white suit we trained in. When someone was told to take me to the *dojo* and show me how to *rei* I was even more wonderstruck, but it simply meant showing me the training hall, and how to bow when entering or leaving.

I learned much more that week. There were meditations, lectures, discussions, demonstrations, mantra, palmistry, astrology, Chinese dancing, acupuncture, macrobiotics, *sumi-e* (ink-brush painting), aura reading, and Japanese poetry. There was even yoga, and that elusive essence that nobody "learns" and nobody "teaches," Zen.

With so much to take in, how was there still time to do so much hard physical training? Every moment was packed. We lived in our training suits day and night, and slept in the *dojo*. Every moment, waking or sleeping, I was absorbed in karate. For the first time, it spoke clearly to me, and what it said was powerful. Never before had my mind and body experienced such a deep and thorough upheaval—from early morning to late at night. It drew together my whole life—not just the previous ten years—and put it in front of me in one picture. It gave everything that had happened, good and bad, a significance.

Having been initiated at the "deep end," in an advanced karate course, I had to go on, but wondered how since all the Okinawan style *dojos* were too far away. I eventually started training again but in a different style which concentrated on the physical aspect only, but having the Mushindo school teaching as a foundation, it gave meaning to what had seemed so meaningless to me before. The door had been opened, and though I was forced to close it I kept in contact with my original teacher and began to relate every happening in my life, big or small, with that teaching.

Training, and eventually teaching, in England and other countries brought me into contact with yet more styles, which showed me again that it is not necessarily the style that is important, but the attitude of the instructor and the way of teaching. Some styles are hard, solid, and strong, and others are soft, flowing, and fast; yet there is no best way. Regardless of how hard or exacting the training may be, it should be enjoyable, satisfying, and regenerating. It should require much from you, but give so much back, although this probably won't be apparent at first.

I do not claim that karate is for everyone, or for all time, or the only way; it just happened to be my path for that time. Anything—yoga, dancing, fencing, archery, archaeology, gardening, or plain down-to-earth everyday living—may be a path of discovery.

The following collection of stories and snippets is the fruit of the ten years I spent traveling in Asia and the many years I have practiced karate and yoga. No special training is needed, however, to understand the tales. Though set in ancient times, they are still relevant today. If we listen, the ancients will still speak to us.

Acknowledgments

I would like to offer my deepest thanks to all the teachers I have ever had, past and present, east and west, meditative and physical, and in particular to Shifu Terry Dukes, who brought both the physical and meditative together within me in a very special way.

My warmest appreciation I also express to Pat Cull-Tucker, who did so much more than type the final manuscript. Her comments, opinions, suggestions, and questions were invaluable and matched only by her patience and interest in the text itself.

Finally, I extend my grateful thanks to all those friends who in any way, helped, supported, and encouraged me.

Introduction

In India in the sixth century, there lived a Zen teacher and Buddhist monk called Bodhidharma (Daruma was his Japanese name). Said to have a fierce countenance and piercing eyes, Bodhidharma was no ordinary monk. He trained in a form of Buddhist self-defense yoga called *Vajramukti*, practiced by the warrior caste of India to integrate mind and body. Bodhidharma's knowledge was deep, but when he left India to travel to the south of China, his teaching was not accepted by the Chinese emperor, whose understanding differed on certain subtle points of Buddhist doctrine. Undaunted, Bodhidharma left and made the further hazardous journey to the north. Robbers and murderers, some who even killed monks to steal their religious relics, were everywhere. That he arrived safely was, in itself, a tribute to his skills. When Bodhidharma arrived at the Shao-lin monastery, he knelt in front of a bare cliff face in meditation—and, according to legend, stayed there for nine years.

Statues and paintings discovered in India show that a system of fighting without weapons, similar to karate, existed at the time of Buddha. The earliest forms of fighting in India are known to go back three thousand years.

So, while it can be said that Bodhidharma was the founder of various fighting systems and the father of karate, it should also be considered that he consolidated what was already known, adding his own vast and beneficial teachings. The greatest of these teachings was his gift of Zen.

When, after his lengthy meditation, Bodhidharma began to teach at the monastery, he changed his methods, for he saw that in its purely contemplative form, the Buddha's teachings were difficult for monks and aspirants to grasp. With the knowledge of his early form of dynamic yoga, he taught a system that related physical movement to cosmic movement, and the power of *ki*, the same energy that is manipulated in the practice of acupuncture. He devised physical exercises in formal sequence, in Chinese called *hsing*, or in Japanese *kata*, to reach the mind through the body, as a form of moving meditation. The monks progressed. One of these *katas* came later to be known as *sanchin*.

Even today, the *sanchin kata* combines some very dynamic breathing with tension and relaxing of the muscles, particularly those of the abdomen and solar plexus. How much more powerful it must have been when Bodhidharma himself originally taught it!

Of the many legends that grew up around this exceptional character, my favorite tells of his being so angry with himself for falling asleep during meditation that he cut off his eyelashes. They fell to the ground and grew into tea plants—a definite sign to Bodhidharma that tea was necessary to assist vigilance—hence, the widespread drinking of tea in monasteries.

As China was a dangerous place to travel, the monks benefited from Bodhidharma's physical teachings as well as from his tea. They were able to disarm an attacker, protecting themselves and their religious possessions, without carrying weapons or diverging from the Buddhist maxim of nonviolence.

So that the monks would be prepared for attack at all times, various hand positions of the Buddha in meditation or teaching were used as a basis for self-defense movements. To the initiated, some hand positions (such as an open hand encircling a closed fist), demonstrated by monk guardian statues at a monastery, would indicate the style of self-defense practiced there. Some of these original movements are still recognizable in the *katas* practiced today.

When Bodhidharma's teachings first came to Japan, they did not take hold and eventually died out with their initiator in the middle of the 6th century A.D. It was not until the end of the twelfth century that other monks returning home from China brought tea seeds and Zen to Japan.

This time, Zen took hold and entered Japanese daily life in the forms of flower arranging, landscape gardening, and tea making. Monk dramatists developed the Noh theater form, using masks and slow, deliberate movements from early sacred dance. The priest artists stylized it in *sumi-e*, ink-brush painting, depicting what is by what is not shown.

It also became the way of the warrior, and it was not unknown for a tea master (man of peace) to accompany a military ruler onto the field of battle to calm and still the Samurai's mind before combat. Mental tranquillity, spontaneity, and fearlessness through the physical discipline of their fighting skills, was the Zen warrior way.

In China, different schools emerged, each according to the regional conditions for training. In the north, with its vast, open plains, where walking and horseback were the main means of travel, big lower-body movements developed. In the south, where people lived close together, along the shore or on boats, short, quick, upper-body movements evolved.

Buddhist priests from other countries traveled to China to learn "empty-hand combat." Some took the art back to Korea, where it grew in various forms. Others took it to the island of Okinawa, where it was practiced in secret. Okinawans, overrun by the Japanese in the seventeenth century, were forbidden to carry weapons, and developed secretly the skill of "empty hand" fighting. Soon Okinawa was a dangerous place for a lone Samurai.

Kept a closely guarded secret by the Okinawans, nothing of the Chinese art was written down but was passed on by word of mouth from teacher to teacher.

Anxious to learn "empty hand" combat, the Japanese, in 1917, invited an Okinawan master of the art, Funakoshi Gichin, to introduce it to them. It eventually became modified and lost much of its original Zen spirit. Today, most modern Okinawan and Japanese schools practice karate mainly as a sport. Very few of the original, spiritual schools remain, and those that survive separate themselves from the more commercial organizations and clubs.

One of these surviving schools is the Mushindo style (*Mu-Shin-Do*: meaning the way of no mind), and its European head teacher, Shifu Nagaboshi Tomio, was my first teacher. My gratitude goes to him, not only for his teachings, but also for his ink-brush paintings. After reading the first story in this collection, he proposed that if I wrote more, he would contribute illustrations. They are a delight to the eye, and a beautiful addition to the work. Moreover, the book's title, *Sword of No Blade*, was his suggestion.

The Teacher Who
Never Said No

In the foothills of the Himalayas dwelt a teacher who had never been known to turn anyone away. Of course, in those days, the amount of instruction any teacher would give to a student depended upon the student's dedication and worthiness. An aspirant could walk many days to a mountain or monastery, but how much he learned when he arrived, or even if he was accepted, depended upon his readiness in the eyes of the teacher.

But Dongma, the teacher who never said *No*, was an exception and, as such, was criticized for his indiscriminate teaching of anybody. He felt that people could only learn what they were ready to learn; beyond that, they could not. And if students tired of this process, then they would leave of their own will.

Dongma had no monastery, but he did have a cave at the foot of the great heights to the east. To most people who lived in the area, their high mountain home was nothing special. They had always lived there and had never known anything else. But for Dongma, this was a special place where he enjoyed a sense of his own insignificance

道

and significance. He felt so small as to be nothing beneath their splendour, yet wondrous that he was part of it.

In this region, there was an area called Kham that was noted for its brigands. Not all men from this area were bad; many used their fighting strength not to rob or take life but to protect it. They could be loyal defenders. On one of Dongma's journeyings, he came across four such brigands. As a mendicant teacher, he had nothing for anyone to steal, but even so, he was aware of an unfriendly presence behind some boulders above the path. When he saw them, he greeted the four as fellow travelers and passed on his way.

A little later, Dongma knew they were following him. When they were level with him, he turned and again spoke as if they were friends. They were at first silent, then broke into cackling laughter.

"He couldn't even give us food," said one.

"The earth feeds me and gives water. But I can show you the trees and plants that are good for food," said Dongma.

"We take what we need, ready-made," said another, mockingly.

"Leave him. He has nothing for us," said a third man.

"We could take his life," said the last.

"Then what would you do with it?" asked Dongma. "What use would it be to you?" When they did not answer, he asked, "Is there nothing you respect?"

After a pause, one replied, "We know who you are."

"Then you can find me any time you wish." And Dongma walked on, leaving them behind on the path.

•   •   •

When Dongma's wanderings were finished, he returned to his dwelling and was greeted by old and new faces. All knew they were welcome, for Dongma never said *No*.

When two full moons had passed, there came a visitor whom Dongma recognized from his encounter along the way. "I've come to stay," the man said, with all the assurance of one who knows he will not be turned away.

"Go and learn respect," said Dongma.

"What for?" the man demanded indignantly.

"For all living things."

"Why? Why me? You've never made conditions before; you never say *No*."

"If you are so sure of that, why are you arguing? Go away and do as I say."

Then Dongma sat down and listened to the comforting slurp of butter tea being mixed in the long wooden cylinder.

Angry and confused, the brigand started away.

"Oh, wait—"

"Yes?" Eagerly, the brigand turned.

But Dongma simply offered him bread for the journey.

Furious, he snatched it, threw it on the floor, and stamped on it.

Dongma looked at the man and then at the bread. "What a pity to stamp on so many people."

"I see no people."

"Do you think it arrived in your hands without people? The sower, the tender, the reaper, the grinder, the—"

"It was a piece of bread—that's all."

"Maybe you are not hungry now, but you have a journey ahead, just as that bread had a journey from its seed to your hands."

"I'll remember that—next time I steal some."

"Good. Then you can bring something you've stolen with you."

•   •   •

A whole season passed before the brigand returned.

"I've done what you asked."

"In that case, you don't need me any more," said Dongma.

"But—you said you'd teach me."

"Did I? I doubt it. . . . Oh, before you go, tell me, what is your name?"

"I don't have one."

"Then you won't mind if I call you Mindrup."

But the brigand was not so interested in his new name as in the small boy before them, plunging tea in a cylinder almost as big as himself. He thought he recognized the boy, but he was unsure, until the boy looked back at *him* with recognition.

But before the man could speak, Dongma went on: "The boy found his way here after a meeting on the road. Seems his father beat him, and he could do nothing to please him. Eventually, he ran away. He'd not gone far when despair overtook him; and he sat down and wept, crying that he was nothing but a crumb in the eyes of his father, to be swept out with the dirt.

"His wailing was heard by a passing traveler who told him that even a crumb is part of the whole, and therefore part of the original seed. The boy liked that; it made him feel part of something greater, as if he belonged, though he wasn't sure to what. Wanting to know how he fit in, he ended up here. . . . But I am certain this would not interest you, Mindrup."

Mindrup said nothing, but took the tea the boy offered only with his eyes.

"When you have finished, you must show me something you have stolen," said Dongma.

Mindrup was not at all anxious to finish his tea, for he had nothing to show, despite his earlier boast. In truth,

Mindrup had become so thoughtful about backgrounds and beginnings that it had become an obsession with him. He wanted to know the history of things and people, until he became frustrated at the tangle of his own thoughts. Where did it end? Where did it begin?

When he could delay no longer, Mindrup blurted out, "I have stolen nothing."

"Oh?" was all Dongma said.

"It was not possible. When I knew what the people had gone through to get to where they were, and how they came to be carrying whatever it was I wanted, and why— by that time, I could not rob them."

"Why not? Surely that would only add to its value."

"But don't you see? When I knew what had passed, I knew the future, the hardship I would be inflicting, and it was too much."

"I do not believe you. Once a thief, always a thief. A lie is nothing to a thief."

"I am not a thief and I *am* telling the truth."

"Not a thief? Ha! Why are you not starving then? If you could not steal, how is it you are well-fed? I am sure you haven't taken to honest work."

"It is true. I have eaten. By the time I had finished asking so much about the people, they regarded me as a friend and invited me to share, or they gave me barley meal for the journey. The whole situation changed. Even when I told them I would take their possessions, they thought it a joke and laughed. And sometimes they even offered something I had coveted."

"And where are those items now?"

Mindrup became even more embarrassed. "I . . . I gave them back. I could not take them."

"Go on."

"Well, it was the same thing in reverse. You see, when I try to take something by force, the victim hangs on to it as if it were his life. Well, when I did not take, they freely gave. When they freely gave, I did not want to take. Such contrariness I do not understand. Yet I know that had they drawn back with their possessions, I would have burned to take them."

"Mmmmh," was all Dongma said. Then: "I will be here a while longer. I will give you one more chance. This time do not bring anything back. Simply go away and think only of giving, only of how you can help others but with no thought of reward. Do this for the space of two moons."

·   ·   ·

When the full face of the moon had appeared and waned twice, Mindrup returned.

"Come and tell me of your experiences," greeted Dongma, and with their little friend at the tea cylinder, they sat down to talk.

"Tell me. Was it cold on your journey?"

"Cold? er . . . no, I don't think so . . . well, perhaps, but . . ."

"But you are not sure? Well, perhaps it was hot then. Were you hot?" pressed Dongma.

"I . . . don't know."

"Well, thirsty or hungry then?"

"I really didn't think about it. Maybe I was, so maybe I drank from the streams without thinking, and ate the same way."

"Dear me, then you must have been very tired."

"I always slept well, under trees, sky, or rock."

"Mmmmh, you can't seem to remember much at all, can you? Perhaps you were sick and lost your mind. It can happen. Hot sun or extreme cold, lack of water and food. Poor boy!"

"I did not lose my mind; I did have enough to eat. I just don't remember."

"But why don't you remember?"

"Probably because I was too busy doing what you told me to do," exploded Mindrup. "It isn't easy, giving when you have nothing to give. Sometimes I found food left beside my bundle from people I had helped and whose recompense I had refused. Unless I met someone who needed it more, this I sometimes ate. I could not waste it, and I knew not where to return it."

"And where is your bundle now?"

"I don't have one any more."

"And the cloth, where is that?"

"I gave that away, too. So I have nothing to offer you for my keep, if that is what you are thinking. But I can work."

"There is no need of that."

Suddenly, Mindrup's heart sank, for if he had nothing to give, and he could not work, then surely it meant he had no chance of being accepted after all. Words rose in his throat, but he said nothing. Their cups were refilled and they drank in silence. Mindrup was sure it was all over, though he wasn't at all sure why.

As one last try he said, "I did everything you asked of me."

"I know. You are well on the way now. That is why you do not need to stay."

Gradually Mindrup realized what Dongma had been doing. He couldn't go back to his three accomplices and tell them he had been refused. He had to finish what he had started, and it was this knowledge that Dongma had used to let him learn. Dongma hadn't been saying *No* after all. Yet somehow Mindrup hadn't expected it to be like this.

"Sometimes," said Dongma, "when we get what we want, it isn't at all as we thought it would be. And often, we don't recognize it when we do get it."

Mindrup was both happy and sad. It couldn't be over; he knew so little, yet he didn't wish to be ungrateful for what he'd already received. Perhaps . . . yes, that was the loophole, of course. "Wait. When I said I had done everything you asked, I was wrong. I didn't bring you anything. On that, I failed. Give me one more chance to—"

Dongma, laughing gently, interrupted: "You have done everything I expected of you. If you had brought me something you'd stolen, you could not have done what you said you did. The second time, if you had remembered anything about your own feelings, then you could not have lost yourself completely in the service of others. You did well."

"But I know so little. I mean, if someone came to me, I would not know how to help, what to say."

"You surprise me. Your first student is doing well."

"Student? You jest. I have no student."

Dongma placed his arm around the boy with the tea cylinder.

"But I have taught him nothing," said Mindrup.

"You brought him here."

"I did not. He came of his own free will."

"And precisely what do you think a teacher does, but point the way? He cannot take you there. The aspirant makes the choice for himself. And he chose to learn more of the seed you showed him."

Mindrup was thoughtful. "All right. I see, but . . . but I still know nothing of meditation. You can, at least, teach me that."

"It is time for me to move again."

"Please . . ."

"Ah, you are a very stubborn man."

"I want to know."

Dongma paused. "In three days I will be settled, with my followers this time, on the high ridge on the far side of the gorge. Come to me there. Take the rope bridge across the river. I shall be waiting for you. Oh, and bring me a measure of nettles. But be sure not to sting yourself. I shall know if you do. Remember, just yourself as you are, and fresh nettles."

It was a simple request, if somewhat strange, and to Mindrup, quite unnecessary; but, if that was what it would take for Dongma to teach him, he would do it gladly.

Then Mindrup had an idea. Perhaps Dongma *was* giving him a chance to bring him something. Didn't he always drink Dongma's tea? Well, nettles made good tea, but then again, so did many other things. So perhaps Dongma wanted the nettles as vegetables. But why only nettles, and why bring them? Why not pick them fresh on the other side? It was a puzzle.

Today, Dongma would move; tomorrow, he would arrive; and the day after, he would be settled and ready to receive Mindrup and his nettles. There were two valleys to cross before reaching the rope bridge, so Mindrup could search well for a good crop of nettles.

On the morning of the third day, Mindrup made hand covers with the last of his apparel and went to the patch he had chosen.

Carefully, he picked the nettles and stripped the lower leaves, giving him a good bundle of clean stems to hold. Then, taking the bundle in his bare hands, he set off for the rope bridge.

The gorge was wide and the bridge bounced and swung, but Mindrup kept both hands on the nettles. He knew he must be as sure-footed as the ibex. A wrong step, and he might drop the nettles or sting himself, and gone would be his last hope. He couldn't falter, however long it took. The fact that he could also fall into the raging river and die did not occur to him.

He hadn't been aware of even a breeze before, but vaguely now he heard a great rushing noise. Perhaps it was the river or the wind, but he dared not give his mind to it. Even on firm ground he knew a sigh of relief could be fatal.

Finally, Mindrup was on the other side, but he still would not let up. To fall, trip, or sting himself now! He must keep his vigilance right up to the moment when he could lay the nettles at Dongma's feet.

When Dongma saw Mindrup approaching, he called out to him. But still Mindrup would not be distracted. "Come, sit down, refresh yourself. How was the river?" Dongma pressed further.

Even when Mindrup had finally relinquished his hold on the nettles, Mindrup had trouble dragging his mind from them. It seemed he had thought about nothing but nettles all his life. Whatever had he thought about before nettles? Would he ever think about anything else?

"The river, was it high or low? You must know; you crossed it," urged Dongma.

"How could I see or hear anything when I had to think only of your nettles? I've thought about nothing else for three days—where I would pick them, how I would pick them, when I would pick them, how I would carry them. The nettles were in my mind long before they were ever in my hands, and now I've put them down, my mind is still carrying them."

"Good. This is preparation for both mind and body. A moving meditation is a good way to start."

Mindrup saw that, once again, Dongma had been ahead of him. To both men, movement was necessary: movement as life, as travel, as meditation—movement in all forms.

Dongma never said *No*; equally, he never possessed a student. He kept them best by "giving them away," just as Mindrup had found with people and their possessions. Mindrup needed time to absorb and see his discoveries, and Dongma gave it to him, saying, "You will always know where to find me when you need me".

And from this beginning Dongma was secretly pleased that Mindrup was walking a path similar to his own.

Let Me See

Ishisan lived in the Ryukyu Islands. He worked hard, lived simply, and usually managed to earn enough to meet his needs. He made hats from dried palm fronds.

One year, he barely had enough leaves to lay in the sun to dry. He must buy some from a friend. Feeling the price asked was fair and not wishing to take advantage of his friend, Ishisan gave him double what he asked. The same thing happened with some dwarf trees, palm fans, and chickens. Then one day, the friend asked a higher price than usual, and Ishisan thought this worthy, so he gave him the exact amount, not a fraction more.

"You've only given me a thousand yen," said the friend.

"But that's what you asked," replied Ishisan.

"But you always give more, sometimes double— you've cheated me!" said the friend, and he went away feeling cheated and angry.

The cheated man then went on to buy from a poor farmer, but his method was to drive a hard bargain, paying only two-thirds or less of the amount asked. The farmer

barely made a living but was glad for anything he could get.

One day, in a weak moment, the cheated man gave the farmer what he asked. The farmer thanked the man eagerly, beaming while he wrapped the goods and thought about what he could buy with the money.

"I can see you are happy, surprised, even," said the cheated man.

"Oh, yes!" said the farmer, pleased that he'd made a sale with a reasonable profit for a change.

"Ah, so all this time you have been quoting me prices you never expected me to pay—you have been cheating me," said the man, and he went away angry.

Much time passed, and the cheated man grew sick. When he lay dying, there were few people to give him comfort. Then one day, he had a visitor. It wasn't anyone he recognized, but what did that matter?

"I've brought you something," the visitor said.

"Let me see, let me see," said the sick man.

"You have a lifetime; why are you in such a hurry?"

"Let me see," insisted the sick man.

"This very moment?"

"Of course—would you cheat me out of what is mine? All my life I've been cheated. Let me see, let me see at once!"

And Death stretched out his hand, and the man saw.

Kyudo—The Way of the Arrow

It is New Year, and the streets of Ekoda, on the outskirts of Tokyo, are crowded with people. They stop to drink hot sake and eat charcoaled eel and sushi. All carry arrows, brought from the temple. The arrow—when correct aim is taken toward one's goal—flies swiftly and surely to its mark. It is a far-reaching symbol of hope for the future, and a good beginning to the New Year.

But when Tokyo was still Edo, before it became the eastern capital,[1] the meaning of the arrow was expressed another way.

•   •   •

Under the guidance of their instructor, three student archers went out to practice.

The first archer aimed carefully and directly at the target—and missed.

The second aimed at a tree beyond the target—and hit the center point.

---

[1]The capital of Japan moved from Kyoto eastward in 1868 to Tokyo, which literally means "Eastern capital." Tokyo was originally called Edo, which had flourished in the late 16th century.

The third archer sat on the ground and looked unwaveringly at the point the arrow should reach—and held it.

"Three of you," said the instructor, "and only one hit the target."

"That's because I aimed beyond it," said the second archer.

"I was not meaning you," said the instructor.

"But I missed," said the first archer.

"I did not mean you either," said the instructor.

"But no one else took aim".

The instructor said nothing. He looked at the third student, who had not moved or spoken since they had begun practicing.

Finally the instructor spoke: "This pupil aimed for the most difficult target of all."

"What is this difficult target?" asked the second student.

"A close target is a difficult one. To see properly, we need distance. His aim was himself."

> He is the bow
> He is the arrow
> He is the target
> He is himself

• • •

From today's arrow-carriers, with their thoughts symbolically on far-reaching goals, the ancient expert archer who never missed his target had achieved inner unity that put him in tune with the bow, the arrow, and the mark, so that they were inseparable—not just once, but every time.

The Poor Man

There was once a poor man who spent his life door to door, village to village, in a high mountain valley, proffering his begging bowl for alms with the words: "I am a poor man . . . " No matter what he received—clothes, sometimes even a fine robe—sandals, food, money, his cry was still the same: "I am a poor man . . ."

As people came to know him, he became part of the local color. He was everyone's "local beggar," and he enjoyed his title. It gave him a place, made him feel that he belonged.

One day, a stranger passed through the village. On his way, he stopped to ask the people about the idle rich man who was sunning himself at the outskirts of the village. They were all puzzled. "We have no rich men here," they said.

"We have a beggar," joked one person, laughing.

"This was no beggar. He wore fine robes, had good sandals on his feet, was well fed, was not working, although I confess I saw no horse."

The people were still puzzled and asked the stranger to describe the rich man. As the stranger began, the beggar came down the street toward them.

"Well, here he comes now," said the stranger, "so you can see for yourself."

The people began to laugh. "Why, that is no rich man, that is our beggar."

It was the stranger's turn to laugh. "A beggar, dressed so richly? You jest."

"No, no, you don't understand. We know him. Those are not his clothes; he wears anything anyone gives him. Underneath, he is just a beggar." Everyone agreed and laughed at the absurdity of it all.

"A beggar in rich man's clothes, eh?" the stranger queried.

"Exactly—can't you see his begging bowl?"

"I can also see his money pouch. It is fat."

"Well, of course, we give him money too—not much, but he spends it frugally."

"He can afford to if he gets everything given to him."

"But remember, it is his life's savings, for he has been begging for a long time now, ever since I can recall," said one old man.

"Then perhaps someone should tell him he is no longer a poor man so that he can stop this masquerade."

"But he isn't masquerading. Truly, he is a beggar."

"I don't know who has placed the heaviest burden on him, you or himself, but the burden is long overdue for a change."

With that the stranger rode on, leaving behind some very disillusioned people. To accept the stranger's words was to admit they had been cheated, but by whom? Themselves or the beggar?

As for the beggar, fear of the unknown had kept him in his place. He knew only begging; he had never given anything to anyone. Now his one dream of being a rich man which he had convinced himself could never happen, had been fulfilled. And he wasn't ready for it. Without a dream, he realized that he *was* a poor man, but who would believe him now? And he couldn't start again in an area where he wasn't known, as new eyes would see him as the stranger saw him.

Now the words the stranger spoke when they first met outside the village traveled back to the poor man on the wind:

Know your limitations,
But do not be limited by them.

The Game

Wu Lan and Li Te were good friends. Li Te was older than Wu Lan and felt a big brotherly responsibility toward him. Li Te taught his friend the long and complicated game of Go, and the two friends spent many hours together in Li Te's garden poised over the checkered board in mental battle.

One day, Wu Lan was late, and Li Te decided to go look for him. Li Te found his friend shuffling along a rutted lane, head down, eyes glued to the ground. Occasionally, Wu Lan peered into a ditch, prodded at the hedges, or kicked over a clump of mud.

"What have you lost?" asked Li Te.

"Mmmmh?" breathed Wu Lan absently, without raising his head.

"What have you lost, Wu Lan?" repeated Li Te, wondering if indeed it could perhaps be his mind—momentarily, of course.

"Nothing."

"Ah, but . . . how can you lose nothing, when you are looking for something? You must have lost something."

"Well, I'm looking for something I've never had, so it's nothing I've lost."

"Perhaps I can help you," said Li Te. "What is it you are looking for?"

"Questions."

"Questions?"

"Questions to my answers."

"But your answers already have questions. That's what makes them answers."

"True, but you see, I am beginning to question them."

Li Te fingered his thin, wispy beard. If his friend continued his quest this way, he might never see him again. Wu Lan could travel to the ends of the earth; he might search forever. Without a word, Li Te turned Wu Lan around and took him to his garden. The Go board was ready for play.

Wu Lan, out of deference to his elder, made no protest. Diligently, thoughtfully, he placed his first stone, just as Li Te had taught him.

He waited. Then, after some moments, he looked up at Li Te, who was still sitting in front of an empty section of squares—empty, that is, except for something Li Te deliberately placed there: a knobbly lemon.

The two men looked at each other. Li Te had a knowing twinkle in his eye—and Wu Lan began to laugh. He laughed all along the hedgerows of his mind, down valleys, and over hills, outward and onward in a great and ever-widening circle.

The question is . . .

Ti Leung Was a Blind Man

Ti Leung had only one son, but the son could do nothing to please him neither inside the house nor working the land. He was a quiet boy who wanted to please his father, but who was so much happier in the woods with the animals and birds, where he was constantly drawn.

This angered Ti Leung who finally turned the boy out. "If you are so happy in the woods, you can stay there," said the father. "You are no use at home, not even to your mother."

· · ·

As time passed, the boy waxed strong into manhood, living off the land in the wide open. He met few people. The animals were his friends, and they understood one another.

One day, a blind man stumbled by, bruised, bent, and scarred from his encounters along the way. The young man helped him, bathed his wounds in the stream, and talked to him just as he spoke to the little creatures, in a soothing, gentle voice.

The man mumbled and chattered and made hardly any sense. Then he slept. When he awoke, the boy brought him food. The blind man was grateful, and after he'd eaten, he began to talk about himself.

Once he had eyes, he told the young man, and once he had a wife. That was many years ago. Now he had nothing, and he was old. He had no friends. His wife had died, and it was then that he had gone blind. Slowly at first, and then more quickly. People told him his children should be his eyes now, but he had no children.

The old man paused, partly for breath and partly to grasp an idea that teased him. He let it go, it was too elusive and he was tired, yet he knew he wanted it. Perhaps it might come back.

Then he said, "If I had had a son like you—ah! I would be so happy. You are a good boy. Your father must be very proud of you." And with a deep, searching sigh, the blind man sank back into slumber.

He stayed with the young man, who looked after him, and they became good friends, for the young man was all the home he had.

"You know," said the old man a few weeks later, when he was feeling better, "I never had a son to leave anything to, but what little I have left in the world is yours. You have been like a son to me. What I have is of no use to me now." He looked down at his meager possessions with unseeing eyes, then asked, "What is your name, my son?"

"As I told you before, I have no name. It is so long since anyone used my name that I cannot remember it."

"Ah, yes, so you said—but tell me, what is your father's name?"

"My father's name?"

"No matter, no matter. From now on you shall have my name, Ti Leung—yes, Ti Leung."

"Ti Leung . . . Ti Leung," repeated the boy, bewildered as he let the name ring on his lips, striking a long-buried memory. "But, my father . . . long ago . . . "

The old man sat up and received his eyes.

His son had ceased to exist for the old man from the moment he had turned him out. Since then, Ti Leung had been childless; then wifeless; then homeless. Now he had so little to offer, but even that was too much for the boy. "Thank you, but there is nothing I need. All I have ever wanted is here," said the young man.

The old man sighed heavily. "I know, my son—but I needed to lose my sight in order to gain it. When I had my eyes, I was blind. You are indeed my eyes now."

Ti Leung lowered his eyelids and died happily, his son's words singing in his ears: "All I have ever wanted is here." And the old man felt wanted.

Breaking Through to the Land of Learning

In breaking tiles, bricks, or wood, one aims *through* the object, not at it. The object to be broken is not the target but merely an obstacle in the way of the target. An aid to understanding the principle of striking through the target in combat, it is also symbolic of breaking through the barriers one encounters in life.

•　•　•

Lobsang had traveled far seeking the land of Great Teaching, which he had heard of and wanted to see for himself. But when he arrived and enquired, "Is this the land of Great Teaching?" he was greeted with only a grunt and a blank eye. He asked again.

"Can you not see?" said the owner of the blank eye, who never answered a question except with another question. If he gave out information, his students would become as "wise" as he, and he was afraid, for he knew nothing about teaching. Never answering questions meant he was never wrong, and thus he was protected.

All Lobsang could see was an island not a mass of land, which he knew it to be. It was as if he were cut off by an invisible circle that he could only feel. He shuddered. The students trained hard and rhythmically under the direction of their teachers, but there was something wrong. Despite the heat generated by their bodies in movement and energy, the place was very cold. He wondered if they, too, would be cold to the touch, but he could not reach them. "Perhaps," he said to himself, "since they move together as one body, there is a communal center. I must find out."

The students trained in serried rows, and he with them, gradually, consciously, working his way to the center of them. But the harder he worked toward the heart, the colder he got, and the more disillusioned and frustrated he became. Still, he did not give up. He wanted to learn. He persisted, but he did not progress. Something was restrictive, and limiting about the teaching and it showed in their way of training.

Suddenly, it was as if he had been turned inside out. One moment he was standing on the brink of the center— and the next moment, he was on the outside again. For there was no center, only a deep void. He was on the edge of nothingness. This great body of people was totally heartless, as if a monster had eaten away the core.

Surely the individual hearts of the students were capable of reaching out and awakening this huge emptiness of their core? Lobsang looked at his fellow students for an answer. They punched and kicked in unison, responded to the commands as one person and intoned *ki-ai* with one voice, but there was no communication, no thread—just isolation.

Anyone with a center had found nothing to feed it on. Each time a heart reached out and was rebuffed, a little part of it died. The dying process was almost complete. Here was a discipline practiced without understanding or compassion. Lobsang wanted to jump into the center and fill it to overflowing with life. But the students could no longer feel. The harder they trained, the colder they and the land became.

One day when the snow lay thick on the ground and training was at its most difficult, one by one the students died. Lobsang watched but could do nothing. They had been destroying themselves for too long, blindly following a hollow teaching.

When they all had frozen to death, Lobsang sadly left. The chilling circle that cut off the Island of Teaching from the mainland had become a river of ice. He crossed it.

Halfway across the river, he stopped. He thought he heard a cry, and he listened against the noise of ice driving into ice over the tumbling, galloping river. At first, he could not see anyone, but then he recognized the shape of a woman, hardly discernible in a white flowing robe against the icy whiteness of wind-polished snow.

She was scarred, battered, and bruised but still alive. Discarded, ignored, and finally cast out, she had been left for dead. Lobsang knew her, and he also knew why she was there.

She was the inner nature of all things, she was the seasons, she was the essence of life, she was life itself. To the "islanders," feeling was weakness. And their fear had brought her to this sad state. They were unaware of the gentleness that only true strength can offer without fear.

When Lobsang freed Life from her icy prison, he begged her to move on with him, but she would not. "There is much to do here," was all she said.

Life stayed and melted the snow. Flowers appeared and buds opened. Soon, she was joined by Spring. They fed each other and grew. Later, others came to the island, but it was not an island any more. The icy river no longer cut it off. Everything was one again—except now the Land of Teaching had become the Land of Learning.

As for Lobsang, he knew he had received the teaching, endured, and survived its rigors to the limit. Now having broken through to the other side, he was at the True Beginning.

The Warrior Spirit

There was once a teacher who found it hard to keep a balanced stance. An overly proud man, he did not realize that his difficulty was his heart of stone. He knew something was wrong, but what? And who could he talk to? Certainly not his students. As for his friends, there were few enough of those. No, at all times he had to keep his own counsel.

His discontent continued to gnaw and nag at him, until one day, he had an idea. Why not journey to the Land of Warrior Spirits, where no one knew him? There, he should be able to get help without any shame.

His mind made up, he made plans and set off. It was a long and tiring journey, not dangerous, yet hard in its monotony and in the sparseness of trees, grass, water, and food. The terrain was both flat and stony, and he missed the peaks that surrounded his own home.

After many days of travel, he saw in the distance the first signs of habitation: little specks, square dwellings with colored rooftops, marching up a humped road. He watched the scene grow nearer until he was at last level with the first door. He looked at it, hesitated, and then banged loudly on it to counteract his hesitation.

The door was opened by a lovely girl. He was sure she would help. But no, after listening to his story, she shook her head and closed the door.

"Well," the teacher thought, "she evidently wasn't competent." But at the next door he got the same response. "Huh! So much incompetence, and this is supposed to be such a noble realm!"

After he had been to every house in sight and received the same reply, he met an old woman, who was collecting pointed sticks. "Well, no use wasting time on her," he thought. But as he prepared to go on his way, the old woman stopped him in his tracks. Her head was down, and she was mumbling. He could not make out any words, just a continuous sound. Yet, somehow, he knew whatever she was mumbling concerned him.

"What are you saying? Do you speak my language?" he asked.

The old woman cackled, because she spoke everyone's language and appeared to everyone according to their needs. In this way, she had her fun.

"What is it you want?" asked the old woman. "Well, go on, tell me," she persisted.

With an air of martyrdom, he said, "It's my heart— I've worn it out. I need a new one."

The old woman laughed again. "Don't you mean *it* wore *you* out? A heavy heart is a wearing burden to carry. But either way, I cannot help you. I can make your heart softer and lighter, but I cannot change it. Besides, are you really sure you want it changed? You won't thank me for it afterward, I can tell you."

Well, he wasn't going to thank her anyway, but he didn't think it prudent to tell her that before he got what he wanted. Instead, he said, "Of course I am sure. Why else should I leave my students and travel so far?"

"Then, if you sincerely want a lighter, softer heart, I can tell you that you have it already."

"What do you mean—'have it already'? There is nothing different at all."

"Then go away. I cannot help you."

As he turned to go, he toppled over to his right. "You have done nothing but change my heart to the other side," he shrieked indignantly picking himself up. "Oh, you are very clever," he sneered.

"I'd rather be wise," said the old woman.

"What's the difference?" he ranted irritably.

"If wise, I will know how to use my cleverness."

"You talk in riddles—you cheated me."

"Nonsense. Your heart is lighter, that's all. You know it, I know it, but your body doesn't know it yet. It is so used to compensating for the extra weight that now it no longer needs to, it still is. Your body must re-educate itself."

"And how does it do that?"

"With use of your heart."

"But I don't intend using it much . . . I mean, in case I should wear it out again."

The woman smirked. "Fool! The heart is a muscle. The more you use it, the stronger it becomes."

"Yes, and bigger and heavier too, no doubt, so that eventually I will be back where I started."

"Do not guard your heart jealously. The best way to keep your new possession is to be free with it. If you sincerely do this, there will always be enough heart for you, and to share."

But he was doubtful about his hard-earned possession. "Give it away in order to keep it? Ha!" he scorned. And paying little attention to her advice, because he had got what he wanted, and wasn't interested further, he went home—controlling the occasional totter.

The old woman laughed dryly. She would enjoy his return visit. He would be back, for a further change, unless meanwhile he changed his attitude, and his mind for himself.

The woman was right. Before the year was out, the man was back. He looked for the same old woman, and found her picking up the same old sticks, which now he saw were little white arrows. He told her that he had trained his body with all of his heart, but there was still something wrong.

"That is because although you are more soft-hearted, you are still hard-headed, so your heart doesn't stand a chance. You don't listen to it. You are worse than a deaf man, for even the deafest can listen to his own heart. You must change your mental attitude."

"Mmmh, you could be right—" he began, and immediately suffered a violent head pain, for the truth is sometimes painful.

"What's the matter?" asked the woman, as his hands flew to his head.

"Nothing, nothing, just a sharp pain, that's all."

The woman laughed her dry laugh. "That's good, that's good. Growing pains, we call it."

"You mean it gets worse?" he asked.

"It must before it can get better."

"Well, let's get to work then," he urged.

"No, *you* get to work. I can't do it for you."

"But all I've done is to give myself a bad head."

"It was bad before you came. That's why you wanted it changed, remember?" chided the woman.

"Yes, yes, you are right." And another stab of pain hit him, as he spoke, this time between the eyes.

"How long will this go on?" he moaned.

"Until you say the magic words."

"I don't know any magic words."

"Everyone has their own magic. You just need to find it."

"Where? How?—Oh, stop picking up those silly white arrows and help me."

"Without these arrows, I cannot help anyone."

"You said you couldn't help me anyway, so what's the difference?"

"I said that I couldn't do it for you. I can point the way. It's up to you what you see and do with the signs." And she held up one of the arrows.

"All right, all right. Have it your way." As he said the words, a gigantic ball of pain exploded in his head. On seeing the woman's arrow, he leapt onto the path it pointed to. Instantly, he had gone so far ahead that he knew there was no coming back. Painful as it was, he had to go through the barrier.

"You read well," rasped the woman. "That's good. You will soon be there."

But as the pain grew worse, he began to doubt. Perhaps he shouldn't have come. Perhaps this was not the way. Perhaps he was wrong and had been all along. Then all thought was taken from him by searing pain that filled his head to bursting. It stabbed and pierced from all directions and filled him, until he *was* the pain.

He couldn't take any more. The next blast of pain would split him into fragments. "I was wrong," he screamed in agony, now fully convinced.

And there he was—"right" on the other side.

With the final, devastating explosion of pain, he was momentarily blinded. Then his mind split wide open releasing something and making room for something new.

On the other side of pain, he found peace.

In the calm that followed, he began to smile, and he enjoyed the unusual sensation. He smiled at the woman who no longer looked so old, and asked, "Who are you?"

"I am the Warrior Spirit who points the way for travelers to develop, according to what they are ready for."

"Yes, I know that; you *all* are, here. But why you? Why were you the one to help me?"

"Ask yourself. You were the one who chose me."

"I chose you?" he asked, watching as the woman became younger and straighter by the second; she smiled and nodded.

"But I wouldn't know how," he continued. "And anyway, if you'll forgive me, I wouldn't have chosen a bent and ugly creature."

"But that's the point. You did choose me. What you recognized in that mumbling old woman was yourself. You were not aware of it, but I can only reflect what is inside you."

"Incredible," he thought, "to find myself in such a substantial reflection." Yet already, this now beautiful woman was receding into the distance—her work done.

He raised his hand in farewell before turning toward home. It was the trees that brought her last (and her first) words to him—rustling trees that now lined his path, first came the familiar mumbling sound, then the words separated; he heard clearly:

> The future is only one second ahead.
> The gift is the present—which is past,
> Yet is always Now.

The Sorceress Who
Thought She Had No Magic

"What a beautiful day," said a king as he looked out onto the sunlit garden of his palace and watched a rainbow dancing in the fountains. "Ah, to be a poor man now, with no responsibilities, no affairs of state to worry about, just time to enjoy my own family and all nature! How lucky is the poor man: he doesn't know when he's well off."

Outside the wall of the palace, a poor man sat waiting for alms.

"Oh, if I were a king," he thought, "I'd have nothing to worry about. I could walk in the garden and enjoy the sun's beauty, with no family responsibilities to worry me. How lucky is a king!"

That night, a sorceress, who had heard their lament, visited both men in their dreams. She told each of them that they could have their wish: that next morning, the king would become a pauper, and the poor man would be a king. First she visited the king.

"Oh, I can't wait!" said the king, overjoyed. "But why must it be tomorrow? Why not tonight?" for he was a ruler and used to getting things done when *he* wanted them done.

"I shall have no worries; my head will rest easy, and I'll be free."

Then the sorceress went to the poor man.

"Oh, I can't wait!" said the beggar. "Why not tonight?" for he was a poor man and used to taking whatever he could get as soon as it was offered. "I shall have no worries, my head will rest easy on silken cushions, and handmaidens will bring my breakfast."

"Very well," said the sorceress, "but you may only have a glimpse tonight. The real change will come at dawn tomorrow," she cautioned, for she was a sorceress and knew the ways of men.

First, she took the king over the wall, and he watched the poor man, and he was thoughtful. Then, she brought the poor man into the palace and let him watch the king. He, too, was thoughtful. Finally, before she went away, she told them she would return just before dawn.

Both men had the rest of the night to think, and when the sorceress returned, they both asked to stay as they were.

"But I thought you wanted an easy bed," said the sorceress, going to the king and the beggar, in turn.

"Oh, I do, and surely his bed is easier," came each man's reply, "but . . ."

"But what?" asked the sorceress.

"But," said the beggar, "he has so much to organize, so many people to pay and keep happy, and enemies to put down. I am a simple man and know nothing of armies or the safe-keeping of borders."

"You'll learn," said the sorceress, and went to the king.

"Well, you see," said the king, "how could I keep my family in such squalor? How could I protect them and their possessions without guards?"

"But a poor man has nothing to steal," said the sorceress.

"All the same," said the king, "I am not used to such conditions, and neither is my family. They would get sick. Here, at least, is beauty. We could not survive in such surroundings."

The next morning, when the king awoke, he said aloud, "What a silly dream I had last night," and went about his day more happily than he had for a long time.

When the poor man awoke, he, too, said aloud, "What a silly dream I had last night," and started on the day more happily than he had for a long time.

Hearing their words, the sorceress laughed, for she knew she had no magic power to change anyone—or had she?

Sanchin—The Oneness
of the Three-in-One

Once there was a student who should have been engaged in private study and practice but instead had his mind on other things. In fact, he was leaning idly against a wall. Unexpectedly, his instructor came by.

"Where," boomed the teacher," is your *zanchin*?"[1]

"Er . . . ," began the student with not a thought in his head.

"And where is your *fudoshin*?"

The student inhaled deeply, then exhaled again.

"Your *ishin*, then?" persisted the teacher.

The student inhaled deeply once more, and this time, blurted out "In my *sanchin*!"

The teacher was silent for a moment, allowing the student, who was obviously pleased with himself, his moment of triumph.

Then, with a twinkle in his eye, the teacher asked mildly "And where is your *sanchin*?"

The student began to practice.

---

[1]The terms used here and elsewhere throughout these stories can be defined as follows: *Zanchin*—alertness in each moment; *Fudoshin*—balanced non-movement; *Ishin*—soul/spirit; *Sanchin*—a dynamic moving meditation in a particular stance of the same name (See the introduction for further discussion of this term.)

One Man and Himself

Two merchants, both having studied the arts of kendo, aikido, and kyudo, stood looking into the same lake.

One man looked at the surface of the lake, while the other looked through it.

"My view is deeper and wider than his," thought the merchant who was looking through the surface. "I can see so much more."

The merchant who was looking at the glass surface of the lake thought of nothing. He was simply reflecting, centering, being.

When the outer eye looks at the inner eye, it becomes the third eye?

The Bored Student

"Master, what must I do to attain enlightenment?" asked a bored student, who had nothing special to do that day.

"Do the impossible," said the Master.

And the bored student went away, bored.

• • •

With the freedom to do what you like—be sure you like what you do.

Compassion—Preserver of Life

Two enemies of long-standing crossed each other's paths on the Sinkiang Plains. A fierce fight ensued. Both men were strong and skilled, and travelers stopped to watch.

When finally one fighter fell bleeding, injured almost to death, the other paused, breathed deeply a few times in the direction of the injured man as if to instill life into him, then dropped to his side.

He began tending his enemy's wounds and healing him with the compassion and love he felt for all humanity. The dying man knew this was no trick, because being old enemies, they had often fought before and knew each other well.

Some of the bystanders were puzzled. Why didn't the victor finish him off? Why try to help him after doing everything possible to kill him?

Finally, one of them asked, "Why, sir, do you now help this man when a moment ago you were both trying to kill each other? Does it mean that death takes away enmity?"

The victor shook his head, but said nothing.

"Then, why?" pressed the bystander.

"Because I respect all life. This life just happens to have a name," answered the man, who had buried the fight on the battleground, at the point of the final blow.

Never had he fought to destroy life, only to preserve it—his own or that of another.

Zanshin

Words often get in the way
    of true meaning.
What is most profound and significant
    is communicated in the unspoken.

When you love someone,
    you look into the eyes, searching.
When you help someone,
    you hold the eyes, sensing.
When you fight someone,
    you do the same, and search the soul.

•   •   •

In a competition fight between two worthy *sensei*, their
unspoken communication was more powerful than their
blows. After the competition, one of the *sensei* confirmed
their silent conversation within their physical exchange.
With love, respect, and concern, the two men "knew" each
other through combat.

A student of both yoga and karate—whose every action exuded peace and gentleness—once said that he always looked into his opponent's eyes first and silently told him "I love you, and don't want to hurt you, so don't make me." If this was not picked up, or it was, but the opponent still wanted to fight, then the yogi would use his strength to defend his softness. With his eyes still holding his opponent's, he would fight with everything in him, so as not to prolong unnecessary violence.

Engaging in eye-to-eye combat—holding the eyes to unnerve one's opponent—drawing an adversary to strike first is one way. But the same skill can also be used to make a contestant inscrutable. There is no communication. Thus movements are never telegraphed and the opponent is kept guessing.

The Mind of the Body

In a village on an island in the land where Edo flourished, there lived a man who arranged his life so that he would not have to think. He was convinced of the merits of a rigid discipline in order to utilize every second of life to its fullest. Thus, he conducted his life according to a strict pattern and brought his children up the same way. As if already conditioned, none of them dared arrive in the world late—a fact he put down to the well-regulated and rhythmic life his wife led.

The marriages of his children would naturally be arranged—without any problems. Death was considered a necessary interruption, granted a brief time for mourning, with a limited display of feeling. Then, for the sake of everyone, neighbors and friends, smiles would be worn by all.

In their orderly lives, there were set presents for set occasions. No one spent time thinking about what, when, or for whom to buy. There was a mode of action—a reply, a smile, a bow, a response—for every possible situation. For special occasions, there were set menus.

Etiquette, at all times, was strongly emphasized for the smooth running of household and social affairs. So, even though a gift was expected, etiquette deemed that the recipient act delighted, surprised, and gracious, but not too effusive; just the required amount of emotion to suit the moment. Even what to wear was never cause for discussion or argument, for a mode of dress was also laid down and followed, cutting out the time-consuming question, "What should I wear . . . ?" Laundry, garments, and celebrations were synchronized.

Nobody was ever late; nobody ever forgot—anything. If anyone was sick, their body rhythms would respond to the stimulus of time, habit, and association, and with very little effort they could carry on inside the splint of automation. Should anyone be inconsiderate enough to be so ill that even their built-in reactor could not function, then provision was made to absorb his or her duties.

With so many points of dissension removed, and no time for differences anyway, to an onlooker everything was peace and contentment.

Then, one day . . .

•   •   •

The father was inspecting his son's studies when he came across some beautiful brush drawings. Achieved with the minimum of strokes and ink, he knew the pictures could only have been done in one concentrated flow, no breaks, for the lines ran in complete harmony.

The man was astonished. How could his son find time to do such work and complete his studies? There was no doubt he had done both, for he recognized his son's *hankow*, or seal.

"What is the meaning of this?" demanded the father.

"They are mine, Father."

"I know that, I know that," replied the man, impatient with the time lost in discussion.

His son made a brave attempt to explain, for in his home, the four main things to fear were lightning, fire, earthquake, and Father.

"I taught you discipline for strength. Your work is good, but how did you find the time?"

"It is difficult to explain, Father," began the son.

"Then start at once and be brief—enough time has been wasted already."

"The discipline you have taught us is strong. It acts like armor, holding us up when we are unable to hold ourselves up."

"Yes, yes, go on."

"Well, I have found it holds my body to its routine without thought, as if my body has a mind of its own and acts independently. This leaves my mind free to wander at will. It can fly anywhere. It can create."

"But you could only have painted during your study time, and that would have left you no time for your school work."

"No, Father."

"No? No?" and the father realized that, in his excitement, he was repeating himself, wasting precious moments.

"It is true that I did the actual painting during my studies, but that took no time at all. The creative part took the time, and this I did while my body worked. With a free mind, I painted mentally; then, all I had to do was transfer my mind to paper during my study time."

"Are you telling me that you worked mentally during your physical activities, and then physically during your mental activities?"

"Yes, Father," and his father almost laughed an un-scheduled laugh, for he realized that his son had found what he was still seeking.

His son was alive and free in his discipline, while he was still restricted by it.

The Man Who
Lived When He Died

A young emperor, who was brought to rule at an early age, worried about his ability to create an aura about him. He couldn't weld the people together under his magnetic personality, for he didn't have one. Loyalty through fear then? How could he make them respect him, and think he was something special?

There was no one he could ask, for he must have no friends if he was to dominate his people, and his advisors must also come under his thumb.

One night, the emperor dressed as a beggar—which he thought was the safest way to travel—and he slipped away from the palace. He sought an answer on a volcanic island in the south, ruled by a shaman.

The emperor told his story to the shaman, who listened without interrupting. Then he advised: "It's simple. You must wear a mask. Keep your own face hidden from the people at all times so that they cannot know with what force they are contending. Keep your distance, and they will think you are stronger than you really are. They will fear you because they will not know you."

The emperor couldn't believe it was really so simple, but already he was beginning to feel better. Eagerly, he asked, "Where can I get such a mask?"

"If you really want one, I can make a mask for you specially molded to your features."

"Good, good . . . How long will it take? I have already been away from my people for a few days."

"You may have it by morning—but for a price."

"Of course, of course! How much?" The emperor was willing to pay almost anything for such a prize.

"The price you must pay is that you must never smile. If you do, the mask will crack. You can sneer and curl your lips in contempt. You can wrinkle your nose as if your people are just a bad smell beneath it—but you can *never* smile."

"But who will see if I smile to myself behind the mask? No one!"

"Oh yes, they will! You cannot relax for one moment. You must always be on your guard against such reactions, for they will surely come through, and *poof!* Everything will be ruined."

"Hmmh," the emperor thought, "it wasn't such a high price after all." He rarely smiled anyway for there was nothing to smile at.

"Is that all?" asked the emperor, still hardly believing his good fortune.

"There is one more thing," continued the shaman. "Once the mask is in place, you can never take it off."

"But you said that if I smile, it will crack; surely then it will fall off!"

"Yes, but by then you will be dead, for my workmanship is such that you will wear it as part of you. Naturally, if it breaks, so will you."

The shaman began to fan the fire with huge bellows in preparation for the smelting of the mask.

"Will it be difficult to wear?"

"For you, no. You are young and will wear into it quickly. Soon you will forget that you were ever without it."

"Will it be a very tight fit?"

"Very tight, so do not worry about laughter, for there will be no room for that. The smile is all that you must guard against."

"Will the mask do everything for me?"

"There are a few more things you should know, but I can tell you about them while I work."

The shaman sorted among his collection of pestles and mortars, shapes and diagrams, instruments and papers, colors and prisms. Finally satisfied that he had all that was needed, he picked up the bellows again and gave a last blow at the fire, which leapt into passionate life.

The shaman resumed his instructions to the young emperor: "First, remember that the surest way to become a big fish is to swim about in a little pond. Second, you must never leave your territory—never let your people know what it is like to be without you. Soon, they will come to believe that they cannot do without you. They will be afraid to be alone and afraid to be with anyone else. You must pull their lives through a narrow tube—put blinders on them, if necessary.

"Never let them know anything else that they may compare to your rule. They must be totally convinced that no one can surpass you, or you will collapse as if you were a puff of wind.

"Don't spread your wings either. Make a big noise in a small space. Draw a circle around you and stay inside it, holding on to your people tenaciously. Should one show spirit or have ideas of his own, belittle him, put him down. Should anyone ask questions, ridicule them, never answer. And, finally, don't try anything new; stick only to what you know. Outside of your own territory, you will be as nothing.

The young emperor began to have a little twinge of fear and excitement as the mask took shape. And, as the work went on into the night, he began to think of the morning, when he would wake a new man.

When it was ready, the shaman fitted the mask for him. The instant it touched the emperor's face, it adhered so completely that his body swelled to match his surly countenance.

"When you get back to your palace," said the shaman, "go to your bed and sleep. When you awake, it will be the morning following the night you left. All this will be as a dream."

Well pleased with his night's work, the emperor stood up and strode away, declaring, "Now my people will see the *real* me."

When the emperor awoke the next morning, the first thing he did was to go to the mirror. The shaman had certainly done a good job. No one would be able to tell it wasn't his own face, and as long as he didn't laugh or smile, no one would ever know. He felt safe inside his mask.

• • •

Throughout his reign, the emperor followed the advice of the shaman with unbending discipline. His was a reign of little joy or laughter.

When age eventually confined him to his bed and he felt his life ebbing away, he feared that the people close to him would see him as a feeble old man. He wanted to die while he still had some of his dignity and his wits. Recalling the words of the shaman, he tried to produce the minutest smile.

Nothing happened at first, so he tried again. His face felt stiff and unpliable. It was strange, but he tried again. Perhaps it wasn't enough; perhaps he needed to try something a bit more ambitious, like a laugh. It was hard work.

At last, he forced his jaws apart in a partial laugh, and a fierce pain cracked across his face. Wanting to make a quick, clean exit, he opened his mouth even wider and forced another choking laugh. His face felt rusty, but he persevered. Gradually, laughter spread to his eyes. His whole face lit up for a second, and then wham! Something broke.

He was free!

At first the physicians thought the emperor was having a fit; surely he couldn't possibly be . . . yet there he was, laughing and laughing and laughing. Once started, he laughed so hard he could neither stop nor catch his breath.

It was no longer forced laughter. He was really laughing with his whole heart. For he knew now that if he had not cracked his mask before death, he would have died without ever having lived. In his new found freedom, he realized that for all these years, he had not ruled or been in control of anybody. He had, himself, been controlled— by his own mask which had enslaved him and his people. Into these last few seconds, he had to pack a lifetime.

Making a Memory

The day was warm and still. Nothing stirred. A faint hum and buzz were the only sounds of moving life. The road wound upward round the hillside. At the side of the road, on a rock, sat a man as still and silent as the day.

Into the stillness dropped the tread of another man on the upward journey. Seeing the man sitting as if part of a landscape on which the world was holding its breath, the traveler, too, felt compelled to stop.

Time stood still between them. Then, breaking the silence, the second man asked the seated man:

"What are you doing?"

"I'm making a memory."

"How are you doing that?"

"I'm capturing the moment—holding it."

"Do you think it will work?"

"Ask me that question again in ten years' time."

"I will—if I remember."

• • •

Ten years later, on the same road, at the same place, the same two men met.

"What are you doing?" asked the one who had traveled uphill.

"I'm remembering," replied the other.

"What are you remembering?"

"That ten years ago, I sat here making a memory."

"Good. Then you succeeded."

"No, it's not good, because I didn't."

"What do you mean?"

"I can only remember that I wanted to make a memory. I cannot remember what that memory is."

"Perhaps I can help. You see, I remember watching you before I spoke. You were staring intently into the heart of a flower."

"You remember that?"

"Yes."

"But what good did it do? I can't remember!"

"But you did achieve your ambition. You wanted to make a memory, and indeed you succeeded—for me."

"You have the memory? Why? How?"

"Perhaps because I was just looking, and you were thinking about looking. I don't know."

"But I wanted it. You didn't."

"That too, perhaps, is a reason, but together we have captured that time. We share different parts of it, yet between us we have it all."

"Mmmmh. So, I got what I wanted, only not how I wanted it."

"Isn't that the way it usually is?"

And the memory-maker's surprise wore a beard of a thousand years.

The Two Wounded Men

Takashima was enjoying a canter on his horse, in the clean, fresh morning air when the sound of angry voices broke the peace. Drawing toward a fierce-looking crowd that had gathered, he could see from his lofty height the object of their anger—in the center was a torn and bleeding man.

Takashima loathed injustice, and, seeing the man so hopelessly outnumbered, he was moved to help him. Nosing his way into the rim of the crowd, he suddenly stopped in his tracks. Through the blood streaks, Takashima recognized the face of a man who, some years earlier, had done him a grave injustice—an injustice so deep that he still bore the scars.

As he hesitated, the past returned in all its painful clarity to swamp him. He struggled between the bubbles of resentment at the old injustice to himself and the rising bubbles of anger at the injustice of the scene before him. Then, he thought of *The Code of Obligation and Conduct to Others*, which he had been taught to observe since childhood. Finally, he asked what he owed to himself.

In answer, he rode straight into the crowd, scattering it to all sides. Grabbing the man, Takashima raised him up

onto his horse without stopping and rode on out the other side of the crowd and out of the village.

When they were some distance away and the wounded man had had time to look at his rescuer, he asked, "Why?"

"Because I dislike injustice—against me or others."

"But you don't even know why they were angry. Perhaps their anger *was* just; perhaps I deserved it."

"It makes no difference. A crowd rarely has a brain within it. It moves *en masse* without thought or reason."

"He raised me up at risk to himself," thought the wounded man. "He, more than any of those people, had cause to kill me, yet . . ."

"You can get down now," said Takashima. The wounded man got off the horse but, still feeling "raised up," said, "You, of all people . . . why?"

Takashima said nothing for a moment, for he had once had high regard and deep respect for this man—which had caused the lingering pain of his wound. Then he replied, "I owed it to myself to act against injustice."

Both men knew that while balms, herbs, and unctions would help the cuts and bruises of the wounded man, Takashima's wounds would have to heal with no help from outside.

After the two men had gone their separate ways, the wounded man thought how strange that the very seriousness of his injuries had saved his life. For he knew that, had Takashima come across him hale and hearty, perhaps resting under a tree, he would surely have killed him in fair combat. It was the overwhelming injustice of his plight that had saved him.

He thought about all the things he had done in his life, for he had plenty of time to think during the healing process; he began to deem it a privilege to be killed by

Takashima—who, indeed, had the right. He vowed that, when his wounds had healed and he was stronger, he would find Takashima and tell him so.

The wounded man had lost much blood, but he was strong and recovered quickly. As soon as he could ride, he went in search of Takashima.

He was prepared for a long search—in time and distance—but, in fact, it did not take long at all. It was almost as if Takashima had been expecting him, trying to make his task easier. When the man made his salutations, Takashima showed no surprise at his appearance; rather he invited him to refresh himself.

Neither man asked about the other's wounds.

Not wishing to appear rude, the man joined Takashima in leisurely tea-supping, although he could hardly wait for the required preliminaries to finish—so anxious was he to humble himself before Takashima.

At the earliest possible moment, he told Takashima; "Now, take what is yours—my life. You saved it, and now you must take it. I am not worthy of it."

Takashima did not move.

"You must," the humbled man continued to urge.

"Must I? Why?"

"I am now strong enough to die, and I have had time to think and to learn."

"Then we are equal."

"Equal? I do not understand."

"I, too, have learned something . . . from you."

"That you can be true to yourself in the face of injustice? We both know that. It is nothing new."

Takashima went on as if the last remark had not been spoken: "It is your enemies, not your friends, who show you what you value most—by challenging it. I might never have known until it was too late how much I loved and valued the things you attacked."

Takashima looked directly at the man and said, "Can I kill a man for showing me that?"

The two men still had a long way to go before they walked the same path, but now their separate ways moved in the same direction, although the space between them was wide and hazardous.

Kotake's Bath

In the shadow of the spitting, smoking, violent volcano called Aso-Gun, on the island of Kyushu in southern Japan, a farmer named Kotake grumbled about his landlord, Otake, to a passing traveler.

"Otake's such a mean old devil, always giving less than what we ask, even though he knows we ask for no more than we need."

"That's easy," said the traveler. "Next time, ask for more than what you want."

"Oh, we couldn't do that. Anyway, he'd know. You see, we need a new communal bath with at least three feet of water. Can I ask for one six feet deep? He would laugh."

The stranger nodded sympathetically and went on his way, which just happened to take him in the direction of landlord Otake. Soon, the two were in deep conversation, for the traveler was a compelling person and it was impossible not to talk to him.

The traveler told Otake many things about the landlord's life. In the background, volcanic Aso-Gun rumbled and bubbled in emphatic agreement with the stranger's words, as he unravelled Otake's life and laid it before him.

"How could a complete stranger know so much about me?" wondered Otake. Feeling anxious, he decided to start stockpiling some merit for himself. He would start with Kotake: the next time Kotake asked for something, Otake would make sure that he got it in full.

Meanwhile, Kotake was having second thoughts about the stranger's words. After all, what would be the harm in trying? Later, when Kotake petitioned Otake for a new bath, he asked for it to be six feet deep, double what he wanted.

Without question, Otake gave orders for the bath to be built, for he knew that Kotake never asked for more than was needed.

Kotake got his six feet of water. Unfortunately he couldn't swim; Kotake drowned.

He didn't know that he would get what he asked for, but then he didn't know the stranger's name was Karma.

To this day, Aso-Gun lives on in its molten fury.

The Shortsighted Man

There was once a man, short in stature, who was unduly troubled by his lack of height. Even more apparent shortcomings were his temper, his sight and his wealth.

To overcome his smallness, he developed a loud voice, which he used often.

One day, someone suggested he study the martial arts. It would, the small man was told, give him confidence and serenity. The little man liked the idea, and for confidence, he studied hard.

He was taught the importance of a spirit cry, and he learned to shout even louder. "Yes," he thought, "I am definitely progressing. Soon I will be an important person. I will gain recognition."

As his outward cries grew louder, his true spirit seemed to shrink, but no one noticed this, least of all himself, for he thought only of the physical.

He went from strength to strength, breaking blocks, bricks, tiles, with his head, hands, feet, and every possible part of his body—for spectacle, for his personal satisfaction, and for an audience that would bring him riches.

When he decided he knew everything there was to know, he stopped learning, closed his books and his mind, and went in search of someone to try his skills on.

The first man he met avoided combat and went on his way like a true master. And the little man laughed, for he was still very "shortsighted."

The next man was a mendicant monk, and the little man felt far too superior to bother with him. "What can I learn from a feeble, old holy man?" he asked himself.

The third man was even shorter than himself, and the little man began to laugh again. He felt ten feet tall.

"Why do you laugh?" asked the very small man.

"Because you are so small," said the little man, looking at the other.

"But you are even smaller," said the very small man, looking *into* the other.

"What! What are you talking about? Can you not see?" shrieked the little man, incredulously.

"I can see that everything about you is small—your mind, your ideas, your heart—but I grant that your head is big."

"And my ambitions," screamed the little man.

"And your mouth," added the very little man.

"What!"

The very little man now began to laugh. "Of course. Don't you know that the best place to hide a small mind is in a big mouth?"

Because of his short temper, the little man could scarcely keep still. He challenged the other man, "We will match our skills and see who is right."

"I have no skills for you to match," said the very little man.

"Ha! So you refuse to fight."

"I didn't say that, only that I have no training."

"Well, you must know something or you wouldn't have survived until now."

"My only knowledge and training is from life itself." And with this, the very little man put down his bundle and stood up. He seemed to have grown a few inches now that he was no longer bowed beneath his load. Undaunted, the little man faced him and, with all the bounce and bigness he could muster, attacked first.

The untrained man was, he soon found, extremely difficult to fight, not because of his skill but rather because of his lack of it. Everything he did was unconventional. He used techniques that no skilled man would use, yet they were effective. He didn't come in with the kind of long or straight attacks that the little man was used to blocking. In fact, the very little man used none of the formal attacks or defenses.

Though struggling well, the little man was confused. Nothing was working, and suddenly he was afraid—not of any physical hurt, but of himself, because he became aware that he was thinking. Total absorption of mind and body in an action left no space for thought and total absorption was necessary to win. Now, he found himself mentally checking every move he and his opponent made.

He and his fist were no longer one. No longer was he in his punch. His mind was on the outside of everything he did. He could see himself, but in the wrong way. Panicking, he went in, arms and legs flaying, with no focus on anything. He came out again with nothing but shortness of breath to add to his other shortcomings.

He closed his eyes and went in once more. But his opponent wasn't there. The little man opened his eyes. "I am trained, you are not. I know every technique in the book, every block . . ."

"True, you do know many blocks, but they all get in the way of your defense."

"What do you mean? I have read every book there is."

"That's a block in itself. Books don't give you experience. You are fighting yourself as well as me. Break through your own blocks and you will more easily break through the blocks of others."

"What books have *you* read?" asked the little man.

"None. I never learned to read," said the other simply. The little man was still not sure that he understood, so much to his own surprise, he found himself asking, "Will you teach me?"

"No, you already have too much formal training. Now you must live and experience life. That is all the training I have ever had."

Still puzzled, the shortsighted man went away, thoughtful. He began to use his head instead of his mouth and to listen to life instead of shouting at it. Right then Life was saying, "What a man tells you is his; what you experience is your own."

∙   ∙   ∙

He had many more encounters with life and found himself embracing it instead of fighting it. He accepted who he was instead of fighting or blocking himself, and he began to accept others.

And he began to grow.

The Wisdom Tree

In a simple but beautiful garden, a sage sat under a *peepul* tree. He was always to be found in its shade, sitting in what appeared to be deep meditation. Yet anyone could come and speak to him at any time; he never turned anyone away. It was always the right time.

One very sultry day, a young man came into the garden with a dish of fresh curd. He placed it by the sage, who slowly opened his eyes and indicated that the man should sit.

"You are troubled?" asked the sage into the silence.

"I wish to speak of happiness," said the young man.

"Ah . . . ," the sage urged, "and what troubles you about happiness?"

"It is said that we make our own lives and happiness—I cannot see how. My life was unhappy because of people around me; so, thinking my life was in my own hands, I packed my things and moved on. But I was just as unhappy at the next place. I concluded that, since the only thing here that was there was myself, the trouble must be with me. Yet I don't want to be unhappy."

"Not many of us do."

"Are you unhappy?"

The sage smiled and replied, "unhappiness, dissatisfaction, frustration—all these emotions are the basis of change, action, creation; they transform continually."

"Do you mean it's good to be unhappy?"

"I mean it's a time for learning, if you can accept it."

"But I don't like being put down," exploded the young man.

"You are acquainted with the arts?" asked the sage who had, at one time, been of the warrior caste of India.

The young man nodded, for he knew what the old man meant, being of the same caste himself.

"Then you know that it is not being put down that matters, but getting up which, in life, may mean surfacing in a totally different place to where you went down.

The young man was thoughtful for a moment. When about to speak again, the sage raised his hand.

"For a sage, I have already said too much. Any self-respecting wise man keeps his mouth closed—or he ceases to be wise," said the sage with a twinkle in his eye, for he enjoyed talking with people.

The next day, the same young man came again to the garden to talk. But, unusually, the garden was empty, except for the beautiful perfume of the flowers and shrubs. It was a pleasure to wait in such a peaceful place, even if he waited all day.

He walked around the garden and began to wonder what it must be like to spend most of one's life there, as did the wise man. Then, he started to wonder what it would be like to be a wise man and have visitors every day seeking his counsel.

He stopped walking about and came to rest under the tree where he had talked with the old man the previous day. As he sat, he fell deep into his imagination and did not notice that he was no longer alone. Another figure had come into the garden and stood looking at him.

When the young man finally saw the stranger, he was startled. Before he could say anything, the stranger spoke, "I would like to talk to you, please."

"Oh, I think you should know first—"

"Please, I do understand, but I will not pass this way again. I would be honored if you could spare me just a few moments of your time."

"But I'm not—"

"I was afraid I would not find you, and that I would need to leave again without speaking with you. Please don't disappoint me, especially as I must leave again very soon. . . . I beg you."

"Well, why not?" thought the young man. "I wanted to know how it feels to be a wise man and to advise people. Here is my chance. Anyway, the wise man himself isn't here and this man has to leave soon."

The young man decided, for fun, to play the part and be the person the other man wanted him to be. He fell silent, yet when the stranger also remained silent, the young man indicated that the stranger should speak.

Delighted, the stranger began: "Sir, from what I have heard of your counsel on happiness, it would seem that there is nothing we can do to help ourselves, because we are who we are. Can this really be?"

"If you don't know, you haven't experienced it. If you haven't experienced it, wait," said the young man, well pleased with himself for having thought up such an answer.

"Then you will not tell me?"

"I did not say that," said the young man, frantically searching for something he could say.

The stranger waited, and finally the young man said, "The nagging of discontent is the impetus to change; change is movement, and movement is life."

"Movement is life," repeated the stranger slowly.

"Have you ever seen a body on a burning pyre move of its own volition?"

"True," said the stranger, considering. But, though discontent keeps us moving and experiencing ourselves and life, sometimes I have moved away from unhappiness into unhappiness."

"Then the springboard of adversity did not catapult you far enough—you still have further to go."

By this time, the young man was beginning to wish he had never started this situation. He found it quite wearing. "Perhaps," he thought, "he should talk only about what he knew and apply the questions to his knowledge of the art of unarmed combat." Suddenly, he was aware that the stranger was talking again.

"You say that certain things happen to us because we are who we are, and are, therefore, in the place where we are, and that because we are who we are, we draw certain things to us by our reaction and attitude, but—"

"Er . . . if you are acquainted with the art, then permit me to put it another way," said the young man. "While what you have said may be true, it is not what happens to a man that is important, but how he reacts to it. What someone does to you, grades him; how you react to it, grades you; and there can be any number of ways to react according to the person you are at the time that it happens to you."

"Mmmh. Then time, too, is important?"

"Again, you can equate this timing with your art."

The stranger was attentive, and the young man went on, well into his subject now. "As you are aware, many defensive movements are circular, and as the circle of the defense progresses, the action changes; as the tension of the two opposing forces is reached, then released, the circle is continued to completion. Same place, different time, and the seeing and the feeling is different because of the completion of an action."

The young man paused, then went on: "The time the circle takes to return to you may be only the blinking of an eye; in life, it may take years to come full circle."

"Mmmh," said the stranger again, slowly and thoughtfully. "The same thing at a different time is never the same."

"There are many points on the circle," continued the young man, "and many circles—as with the planets, all operating at the same time: complete, yet part of something else."

They both fell silent. After a while, the young man looked up and was startled to see, not the face of the stranger, but that of the sage. The young man was lost as to what to say.

"Do not be alarmed. It is providential that you wished to appear exactly as someone wished to see you. I do the same myself. It is another way of showing and, for the person to whom I appear, another way of seeing."

"But I came here to see you," said the young man, "to ask you more questions."

"And, instead, you answered them."

"Only the stranger's questions, not mine."

"And what are your questions?"

About to speak, the young man's face changed as he realized that the stranger's questions were his own. And he had answered them.

"But where did I get the knowledge?"

"From yourself."

"Myself? How?"

"It was always there. You just didn't know it."

"Why didn't I know it? You did. You knew! You must have known." The young man lapsed into thought. The sage waited, smiling.

"How strange! When I thought I didn't know, I really knew. Now I know that I know, it makes it all different." The young man became excited as he went on. "Yes, that's it! I see it now: when it's the same, it's different, and when it's different, it's the same."

The sage's smile broadened.

"So, maybe I was happier when I didn't know I was happy . . . or . . . or unhappy! . . . which means . . ."

As the young man left the garden, delighted that he understood so well, he thought he heard the sage laughing.

The Valley of Beautiful People

Every spring, Kam Ti looked forward to visiting the Valley of Beautiful People. But every year, something got in the way and stopped him. And every year he was that much older.

He had heard that the valley itself was beautiful and that the people reflected that beauty. More than just a valley, it was really a great, green, fertile bowl, hollowed into the earth's crust, with colorful mountain spheres at the rim. The freshest of smells hung on the air healthy, healing, natural. Down the sides of the green bowl, waterfalls of the purest tasting, crystal water flowed. With a soft swishing that assailed one's ears, the water ran down into a stream, which narrowed and snaked through a modest slash in the bowl, to freely flow outward and onward.

Kam Ti heard many stories about the valley from passing travelers. Some said that cosmic energy flowed into it. Others said all knowledge and goodness flowed out of it, to feed all those who were ready to receive. Some said there was only one way in; others said there were two approaches. Flowing in, flowing out, approaching from the

east or from the west. Kam Ti had to go and see it for himself.

He wondered if this year would be different for him. Would he really make it to the valley this spring? Or would there again be something to stop him? His crops? A sick animal? A sick friend? His own health and strength? Or would it just be necessary chores that took away the time while he wasn't looking?

No, he decided, this year he must go. This year, whatever wasn't finished, he would leave unfinished. Every year that passed made him aware he was that much older and no nearer his goal. He began to doubt that he would ever reach the valley of his dreams. The previous year, he had fallen ill. But not until he recovered did he know just how close to death he had been. Even so, though he miraculously recovered, another year was lost. But there was something hopeful in his sickness, for something had pulled him through against all odds. Perhaps he had been visited by his ancestors or his soul had visited the valley and gained strength. He didn't know, but whatever had happened, he now felt far closer to the valley than before. It felt familiar to him, as if he had actually been there.

Since his quest was so much on his mind, it wasn't surprising that it occupied him while he was delirious, but it was all so clear—hardly the distortion of delirium. He felt he was being prepared; knowledge was being imparted to him in his set-backs. He must use it.

He picked up his staff and felt its weight. It felt good in his hand. His sturdy sandals, too, gave energy to his feet, urging him to stride out. Yes, he would give himself a few more weeks to do what was necessary, and then . . .

This was, in fact, the year Kam Ti was destined to start his pilgrimage. A peaceful pilgrimage, not one fraught with dangers, but nevertheless that's how he regarded his journey. Thus, staff in hand, feet comfortably shod, he traveled frugally, with only a little food, a bowl, and his scrip.

He crossed valleys and rivers, plateaus and plains, high places and low, craggy places and the softest, velvety grass and deep-clustered moss. He saw undulating places of smooth rainbow rock, colorful places overflowing with blossom and bloom, the bluest of blue water against snow laden mountains, that spanned a blue, sun-cleansed sky. There were dark places where trees loomed large with close, knobbly heads that hid deep secrets, and eerie places of unusual night sounds. And there were exposed places and friendly, sheltered places. He loved them all.

The variety of his journey made him wonder: if this was the journey, what would the valley itself and the people who dwelled there be like? The thought spurred him on in his excitement. On the other hand, he had no wish to scurry through the perfumed air. The peace and beauty were thus tempered with a little challenge, in a perfect balance.

Kam Ti knew clearly what landmarks would tell him when he was near the valley, and he had no doubts about recognizing them.

He had been walking and climbing, fording streams and rivers for nearly two months. He felt sure that soon he would see a familiar rock formation of standing stones like a towering gateway leading to a high plateau. Even if he reached the bowl from the opposite side, he knew what to expect. He would again go through a rocky place and then follow a stream steeply down to meet another stream, flowing out from between high rock walls from the floor of the basin. The streams joined there and flowed on unhindered, away from the valley.

Suddenly, there it was—the rock gateway he had been expecting. In awe, he approached the spiring stone slabs and stood for a moment in their presence. Then, he went through. Yes, he was approaching from the high side, along the plateau to the rim. He would walk slowly to it, savoring each step in anticipation.

Ah! He let out a deep, satisfying breath. And in that moment he caught a glimpse of the valley's energy, the flow he had heard about—moving in and out. Yes, like the breath, energy did flow in, in order to flow out and disperse into the beyond. It was a flow of giving and receiving, starting the process even by giving, like the first breath of life. That one deep breath gave him a new insight.

The journey had softly touched his soul, penetrated to his depths. Soon, he would look down and at last see the Valley of Beautiful People. He felt ready, yet he could not imagine what he was about to behold. With every step, he neared the rocky spheres of the rim. At the gap ahead, he would look down at the streams coursing into the bubble. If only he could close his eyes and walk to the edge, then snap them open when he was there! He paced himself to take his time, but he was impatient at the last and flew to the top on winged feet. With a deep, exultant breath, he looked down.

Whatever he had expected, it wasn't what he saw before him. He must surely be in the wrong place. Yet he knew he couldn't be. He knew it too well. He had arrived.

The valley itself was as he expected—but not the people! Not only were they not beautiful, they were ugly! And it wasn't just their faces that disappointed him, but their whole bearing. He had expected tall, regal people, beautiful, upright, moving liquidly; bold, yet tempered with compassion and goodness, sensitivity and joy.

These people, well, they weren't exactly staggering about blindly, but they did seem to fall heavily onto each foot. He had expected lightness, a springy or gliding step. This was all wrong, completely opposite to anything he'd been led to believe. But why? Clearly, what he had been told, the tellers had believed. What they believed, they must have seen. So, what was wrong with him that he couldn't see?

He decided to approach the problem another way. There were usually two sides to everything—an east or west side, even an inside and an outside. From a different angle, he would see another view. See—yes, that was it. They were like blind people, stumbling about and into each other, and yet, as he looked, he saw they weren't actually blundering into each other. There was an order. They seemed almost to contact, then pass on without actually touching. But it was far from what he'd expected.

He started to go around the rim toward the other side. He would look at the puzzle from there. Round he went to the rocky place, then on and down, past the meeting of the two streams, and finally into the chasm.

He was at first struck with a deep tranquillity, an almost euphoric envelopment, just like earlier moments of his journey but magnified a thousandfold. This was the way he had expected it to feel. The valley was beautiful, he felt beautiful—so why were the people as they were? He moved slowly, as if through an enchanted fantasy world. He could see a thick slice of vibrant green at the end of the rock walls. When he reached it, he would be so much closer to the people, on a level with them. Yet he did not feel horrified or sad at the thought; rather he felt ecstatic, as if walking on air.

As the chasm fell away behind him, he was with them and moved among them. They knew he was there, too, although they could not see him, for now he saw that, indeed, they all were blind. They could not see the beauty that he could see, yet they knew it and felt it. And he knew instantly that they had created it.

These people had so strongly imparted themselves to their surroundings that it made it beautiful for all others. He was surprised to notice that there were no children. No one spoke, but they were all communicating. Even as he realized this, a voice that could not be heard with the ears transmitted to him: "There are a rare one or two young people."

The people communicated as they went about their work, lovingly tending the earth. Kam Ti's whole being was brimming over with their fulfillment. The same voice that did not speak to his ears asked him to look again at the people, but to see them as they saw each other. And he did, and he was amazed. They could see—really see each other, from the inside. With their own expanded insight, they saw the true being. Although literally blind to the outside world, what clarity of vision they had! He could see it all clearly himself now, yet not with his eyes, any more than he was hearing with his ears. His senses responded on a different level.

Amazed, he realized that he could see the earth, too, as a body, with all of its suffering and many scars, and the special place the valley held upon the earth's surface. It was like a junction on a meridian, a cleansing lymph node, a recycling energy point, which made even the earth beneath his feet well and happy.

Still, he was puzzled. What was he doing there? What was his place there? What had happened to him? He didn't really belong in the valley; he still had his worldly sight; yet now he was among them as one of them and could see what they saw, hear what they heard. His own sight melted into insignificance. Compared with his new discovery, his worldly senses were a mere introduction.

Again, the voice that needed no ears told him, "You have passed through the gateway to your own potential. The difficult journey that burns the dross yet leaves the pure has brought you here."

Again, Kam Ti was puzzled. "But it was not a difficult journey," he felt himself say.

"For your soul, that is true; but for your body, it was difficult. How much did you suffer before you left your home to find this place? At the most extreme point of your sickness, your body gave up, but you did not."

It was true. He knew. He had been very sick, but he wanted to live and make the journey that was his life's ambition. Being alone, he had to make twice the effort.

"Only one life's ambition?" teased the voice. "Did you not know that your soul made the journey for you?" Kam Ti wasn't sure how he'd managed to do that.

"How do you think you knew so much about the valley, in which direction to go, and what to look for?" He always thought he must have gleaned that information from passing travelers, but now he wasn't sure from whom or when.

"Your journey started long before you set off. That was the difficult part: the troubles you went through each year to reach your goal. The time you enjoyed along the way, as you rightly say, was easy. You even knew that it would be easy. The hardest part was getting started; and that was part of your preparation, which began long before that."

"No wonder," thought Kam Ti, "that children are rare here." But it was good to know that it was possible for them, too, to come. Yet how could so much suffering and struggle be packed into such a small life span? How much pain could so few years hold?

With a humorous lilt in the non-speaking voice, and a twinkle in the non-existent eye, the reply came: "Some children are born very old. We are not concerned with chronological age here."

Kam Ti knew somehow that this was only a visit; that he was not here to stay; yet he also knew that no one left the valley. Perhaps they would expect him to stay. That was something he had not been prepared for.

"You may stay as long as you wish," said the pulse, "but this time, as you already know, is only a visit. You are not here to stay."

Kam Ti was perfectly content. Kam Ti felt so good here, neither hot nor cold, hungry nor thirsty, tired nor heavy, just soothed and relaxed through and through. He stayed and refreshed himself, moving, living, and communicating with so many beautiful people. Whether waking or sleeping, he was light, cool, and cleansed. What bliss! What beauty!

Kam Ti stayed in the valley all summer. He was not even worried that, if he stayed too long, he would never leave, that he would get too used to a life with beautiful people in a beautiful place. The valley was not a place to worry. Worry took far too much effort, and being here was like a heady intoxication.

When the time came for him to go, he knew. His feet urged to carry him once more out of the bowl. He was not sad, neither was he happy. It felt right, and the time was

right. There was a time to come, and a time to go. Yes, he
was blissfully content.

He entered the chasm once more—calmly he reached
the point of two streams, the outer slopes, and the rocky
place. Then on he went along the rim to the far side, from
where he first looked down into the valley.

When he arrived at that same spot, he looked down
once more in farewell. The people were indeed as beautiful
as their surroundings. He had truly walked where few had
gone before, and fewer had ever left. The people still looked
exactly the same physically—bent, stumbling, and blind.
But this was not ugliness; this was beauty. How could he
ever have thought otherwise.

As the standing stones receded behind him, he wondered how long it would be until he could return to stay.
How old would he be? How many thousands of years in
the future? How many more lifetimes? Or, would it be
tomorrow? No, he didn't think it would be the next day,
but it could well be the next life.

The journey back for Kam Ti was a stormy and harsh
one, as the elements of autumn were anxious for winter.
But Kam Ti was glad, for steeped as he was in the aura of
the Valley of Beautiful People, he could go on enjoying it
without the harshness of being pulled through from one
consciousness to the other. He was not anxious to relinquish
the experience of seeing with his body and go back to seeing
with his eyes; though he could see the storms gather and
break, though he could feel the spearing rain and the wet-
ness of the water; though he could taste the breath he
plucked from the air; what his senses told him did not touch
him. The aura of the valley was still the overwhelming force
in his being.

He hoped it would stay long, stay with him in his home. He would try to hold on to it, to feel it, to sense it, to live it, even as time distanced it to a thought, a memory, a dream, until the time came for him to return and stay. Next year? The year after? The year after that? Or the next lifetime? The life after? Or the life after that?

Kam Ti was content. And the more content he became, the more his life reflected what was needed for him to return to The Valley of Beautiful People.

How to Keep Your Face
and Lose Your Head

There once was a bandit adventurer who, as he made his way south, plundered here and there according to his whim. Outwitting people was a great game to him. He liked to shock and embarrass people and watch them squirm. His favorite pastime was intimidating the less fortunate and then laughing at them. His tongue was as sharp as his sword and could cut just as deep into the lives of those unlucky enough to cross his path.

One day, he had worked up an appetite and was looking for somewhere worthwhile to satisfy his hunger. He intended, as he always did after a rampage, to dine well. He didn't have to look long.

Arriving at a Shinto Shrine, he found a meeting in progress in the main hall. It was obviously a special meeting because food was being prepared. Even better, through the partly open sliding doors he could see that the place of honor by the Tokanoma post was empty. The thought of sitting by the alcove where a fine scroll was hanging pleased him. They could almost have been expecting him.

Dismounting, he strode in, straight to the special place opposite the door, and sat down as if he had every right to be there. He bowed, as a formality, and smiled his most charming smile to all.

The priests responded with customary formality, acknowledging his bow and smile. Then, there was silence. No one knew what to do next. After a quiet consultation among themselves the host approached the bandit and informed him, with courtesy and charm, that he was sitting in the place reserved for the guest of honor.

"Wouldn't you feel more comfortable moving down a few places?"

"I see no guest of honor. Where is he?" asked the bandit.

"We are waiting for him now. We cannot think what is keeping him, but he will arrive. He has given his word. Meanwhile, if you would please—"

"Then I shall stay here until he does come," interrupted the bandit.

He had chosen his place, and there he would stay. "Move down!" he thought scornfully. He had never moved down in his life. It was almost a physical impossibility. But he was curious to know whose place he had taken, and what sort of meeting this was.

When, after some time, the honored guest had still not arrived, he demanded to know who he was.

"He is a merchant," they told him, and the bandit immediately burst into uncontrollable laughter.

"A merchant! Ha! All this fuss for a mere merchant?" The bandit was almost insulted that he should be occupying such a lowly place and was contemptuous of these priests for venerating such a man—for, in ancient Japan, the merchants and traders were the lowest of the four classes of people, the highest being that of the samurai.

During this time Japan was undergoing many internal wars. One of the local warlords was stealing rice from the priests, who themselves were no better off than the people around them—who were suffering great hardship in order to pay exorbitant taxes.

When the bandit had ceased his laughter, the host priest told him, "The merchant whose place you have taken has promised to fulfill certain obligations that he imposed upon himself. He is a very wealthy man—we helped him once. In return, he has promised to replenish our rice supply whenever we need it."

"Anything a merchant can do, I can also do, and much more effectively," boasted the bandit. "Whatever amount he offered, I will double." He knew he could always steal it from someone else and enjoy doing it.

Clearly the bandit's arrogance wasn't going to let him move down, no matter what responsibilities he took on by stepping into someone else's shoes; he was even less likely to move down now he knew the place was held for a lowly trader.

The priests made another attempt. "We should tell you that the merchant has promised something else, too."

"And what is that?"

"He was bringing gold to help our people—he is a generous man. That is why we planned this gathering in his honor."

The bandit raised his hand. "Enough. I can give you all the gold you want, and more," he said magnanimously, although, in truth, he was beginning to wish he hadn't stepped so firmly into such a giving man's shoes. But, his pride and arrogance couldn't allow him to go back now.

"But you don't understand. We need the gold now," pressed the priests. "And it is a vast amount," the host added, knowing that no ordinary citizen would carry such a quantity with him.

"You shall have your gold—and have it now, and then you will see that I am more worthy of the place of honor than your merchant."

Already the bandit was planning to steal the gold back from the shrine. But, for the moment, it would buy his honor—his face.

He went outside to his saddlebags and brought all the gold he had plundered into the shrine. When the priests saw the seals on the bags, they knew their merchant had kept his promise, but they knew, too, that he would not be making another.

Feigning gratitude, they inspected the gold graciously. Then, all but one bowed low to the bandit, to which he responded.

The one man who did not bow raised his sword and severed the bandit's head from his body in one blow.

•   •   •

To keep his face, the bandit lost his head; not by wearing someone else's shoes, but by stepping more squarely into his own.

Horizon

He was right, of course: this was indeed his future, and it was no different from his past. All his life he had been driven to achieve his allotted task; yet it was always on the horizon, always out of reach. No matter how fast he traveled, or how long, how wide, how far, he could not reach his goal.

Now, as an old man, he had to admit sadly that it was not going to happen. Taking an honest look at himself, he knew he was no nearer his goal than when he started. But why? Where had he gone wrong?

Early in his childhood, his parents told him what the family astrologers had forecast at the time of his birth— that he had a "special task to perform"—but they did not tell him what it was, nor was he given any tools or other assistance for the job. He was on his own.

He'd been so sure that this was the right direction. What other way could he have taken? But now, it seemed, he had been mistaken.

He realized he was talking in the past tense, as if his life and its purpose were already over, but that was how

he felt—it was finished; he was finished, beaten, devastated, frustrated, dejected, and disbelieving. He looked back on his life and saw it as a waste; a waste of effort, loyalty, perseverance, and trust. What had he to show for his time here on earth, dedicated as he'd been to what was an impossible and fruitless quest?

He viewed wistfully those he met along the way who were charged with no special mission in life and so took each day as it came. Not looking to the far horizon, they looked at what was under their noses, not what was at the end of them, and were happier for it. He knew all this now, and how he wished he had known it sooner, when he could have changed his path or joined his fellow travelers. Now it was too late to do anything. He had failed, and his heart was heavy.

Solemnly, he stood looking across to the far horizon that he would never reach—when suddenly, in an unexpected burst of clarity, he saw that in order to do anything, there must first be life. Had he known the future, he could not have gone on, striving to no end. Thus, his life would never have reached this point. His hope, faith, and a natural trust and optimism had kept him going, brought him to this point, drawing him on with meaning and purpose. To be where he was now was exactly what he needed. This was the point he had to reach, a giving up or letting go, in order to start.

As he stood, silent and still on the threshold of gathering dusk, sky and earth's edge merged in his sight, and he felt their coming together within himself.

Nothing was finished. Here was his beginning.

The Demonstration

In the south of China, along the Yangtze Kiang, there was a small community, the center of which was the monastery. The abbot was an old, wise, and much loved man.

One day, a stranger broke into the peace of the community, his dark skin almost white with the dust of traveling. A rough, worn pouch slung around his body and a stout staff were his only possessions. Through meager garments, his thick brown arms were bursting for release.

In the main square in front of the monastery, he surveyed all around him, as if he were contemplating buying the place and everyone in it.

The people were curious as well as a little fearful, but their curiosity outweighed their fear, and they gathered at a cautious distance to stare at the stranger.

He appeared to be preparing for a demonstration. Perhaps he was a seller of herbs and potions, aphrodisiacs and lotions; perhaps he was a seer—but no, he didn't have quite the manner or attitude of a seer. Maybe he had his own brand of medicine, or a new method of divination, some different attraction perhaps, that they had not seen before.

Spreading his arms, as if to embrace the people, with staff in hand, he challenged, "I am the fittest man in all

China, and I have traveled long and wide in my quest to prove it. I want my superiority to be known and recognized throughout the land. Who will dare to contest me? Who will dare to pit their strength against mine?"

He peered at the crowd which had grown a little thicker now, and he advanced occasionally toward a possible opponent.

Disturbed by the commotion outside, the abbot had come to the threshold of the monastery and was standing quietly unseen, yet seeing.

To stir the people to action, the fit man was now wielding his staff and prodding at a few of the young men.

"You—and you there—what are you afraid of? If you cannot stand alone, you can fight me together, huh? See how generous I am, and still you have no stomachs, ha!"ha!"

Roaring with laughter, he bent down and slapped his thighs. Spinning round and up again to advance on the other side of the square, he caught sight of the abbot who now stood openly in the entrance.

A murmur rang through the crowd as they followed the fit man's gaze, and then, silence.

The two men looked at each other. The fit man, keeping his body perfectly still, moved only his eyes to observe the abbot. The abbot fixed him with his own direct gaze, with just the hint of a twinkle behind it.

Finally, the fit man spoke, "So, old one, you must be someone here. You don't look much to me. Ha! I warn you, I run miles without the slightest effort. I can fight bout after bout without tiring and can outlast the strongest fighters. I am always the last one left standing."

He paused to let his words sink in and to bathe in any admiration coming his way, then, he added, "Will you fight, old one? Do you dare?"

The abbot smiled, nodded knowingly, and stayed where he was, for he had heard it all before.

Slightly irritated but still in control of himself, the fit man scorned, "Then I must find a way to make you." And he goaded, persuaded, coaxed, provoked, and insulted the abbot, but the older man would not be drawn.

Then, the fit man insulted the abbot's students. This was too much. He loved his students and could not leave them undefended.

"So, at last you fight. That is good. How many miles do you run?" laughed the fit man, certain that the abbot did not run at all; and he was right.

"None," replied the abbot. The two men were now facing each other in the square.

The abbot, whose skills and faith would not allow him to attack first, waited for the fit man to attack. This the man quickly did, with a great roar that seemed to shake the ground beneath their feet. The abbot side-stepped adroitly, taking his opponent's target away at the last moment. Then, he countered with the minimum of effort, and the fight was over before it had begun—for the fit man, through the force of his own body weight, lay in the dust.

He sprang up, for physical pain was nothing to him. But the abbot had thrown him mentally.

"That isn't fair," he cried out. "I didn't have time to show you what I can do, and how much I can take, how long I can stand."

"You seem very concerned with quantity," replied the abbot.

"But I want to fight! I like to feel my own strength. You don't even look strong. You can't even run—you said so."

"True, but I practice daily, particularly the formal exercises."

"Hah! You mean, *kata*. Those pretty dances. I've seen them, but they are not for me. I want something of real value. That's why I never practice alone, only on others. What use are formal exercises to me? I want to fight."

"Those 'pretty dances,' as you call them, can teach you something."

"Like what?" spat out the fit man. But the abbot knew that he didn't really want to know. The man would have to learn the value of *kata* for himself in order for it to mean anything. Instead, the abbot said, "Show me an original *kata* that begins with an attack and ends with a block, then I will tell you."

The fit man was silent for a moment, then, "That will take much time. There are many forms and many different schools. If I return, it will be to fight again, old one. What you ask will take too long."

"What is your hurry? You have the rest of your life. And when you return," for the abbot knew that he would, "if you have learnt anything from your search, then not one blow will be exchanged between us. We will not need to fight; we will know each other."

•   •   •

Eventually, the fit man did return, but only to say that he had searched and could not find such a *kata*.

"That is your first lesson," smiled the abbot as they took tea together. "And now for your second: block your opponent mentally, before the attack is born. Always keep your own values and know when to defend what is dear to you. You may even have to know when to protect what is dear to your opponent, but that comes with experience."

Then the fit man knew that the abbot had been protecting him like one of his own students. His first loss had truly been his greatest gain.

The Chasm

When Shin Po rode through what was usually a sleepy village in the region of Ladakh, he was surprised to find a very noisy scene. People were running in all directions.

When he asked the cause of the disturbance, he was told that something had frightened Kwan Li's horse. It had galloped away with him and finally deposited him at the bottom of a chasm of unknown depth. Several unsuccessful attempts had been made to reach Kwan Li, but now, he didn't even answer faintly to their calls. More men were coming from neighboring villages to help.

Shin Po knew the chasm that opened its craggy jaws at the edge of the village. He also knew Kwan Li. Suddenly making up his mind, he dismounted and said, "I will go down."

"But it is very dangerous," they all cried. "No one man can do it alone; we need ropes—strong ropes."

"I will wait for the ropes."

"Excuse me, sir," said one old man, "but you are a stranger here. You do not know the history of this chasm. An age ago, after a very long drought, we awoke to a

terrifying earthshattering rumble that went on and on. During that night, the earth split wide open, and it stayed that way. Nobody knows how deep the chasm goes. Some say it's dry down there. Others think there is water at the bottom of the darkness, but nobody has come up to tell us. Some who have fallen in have been lucky enough to come to rest on a ledge, but as for the others . . ." The old villager shrugged. "Anything could be slithering about down there, born blind in the permanent darkness."

The old villager went on, "Er . . . may I enquire your name, sir?"

When Shin Po told him, the people heard and were very concerned.

"But it is well known that you and Kwan Li are sworn enemies. You cannot want to risk your life to save his. Surely you must want him dead. Er . . . forgive me." The old man gave a polite bow.

"There is nothing to forgive," said Shin Po. "You speak in truth. I do want him dead, and it is for this reason that I must go down."

"But you need do nothing," said the old man.

"If I do nothing, and he dies, it will still be as if I killed him. No, I must go because I am the one who has most to lose if he dies."

Seeing him to be in earnest, the old man said, "Then we will help you." They rigged up a sling that would take the weight of Kwan Li's body, to be hauled up separately from the rope supporting Shin Po. Not knowing how far down he would have to drop in his search, Shin Po asked for rags, oil, and a stout stick to make a torch.

"Are you ready, Shin Po?" asked the old man when the torch was lit. Shin Po was more than ready—either to bring up Kwan Li alive or to die in the attempt.

Slowly the villagers lowered Shin Po and watched the flame from the torch creep down, down, sometimes out of sight, as he went below a bluff in the chasm wall. A dank odor assailed Shin Po's nostrils, as he dropped lower. He wondered if the ropes would reach if he needed to go all the way to the bottom.

Hollow sounds bounced off the walls, but they were indefinable, like echoes of echoes. He seemed to be descending into the earth's center. At one point, a friendly tug on the rope from above let him know the villagers were still with him and letting out rope. But for how long, he mused. At this length, it would be a long haul up.

Several times his feet hit a ledge, but nothing else. Several times, too, he called to Kwan Li, but there was no answering call. The air in the chasm was heavy and close, but at least, with no breeze, his torch was steady. Without it, he hadn't a hope of seeing a thing, so thick and unbroken was the blackness.

Shin Po was wondering how much further down Kwan Li could be, when another tug on the rope told him that all was still well. The walls were now moist—not dripping, but slippery.

Then he felt a sharper tug on the rope, the signal telling him the rope was almost played out. He couldn't fail now—he had to find Kwan Li!

His thoughts were interrupted when his feet touched a ledge, as they had done so many times before, except this time, they moved against something soft. He lowered his torch, and saw below him a still, bloody form—Kwan Li.

He gave the prearranged signal to those above. Shin Po dropped to his side. His enemy was still warm but barely clinging to life. His wounds were multiple, but the most damaging one was to Kwan Li's skull.

Master of many skills, Shin Po was acquainted with the ancient, if violent, form of first aid known as *kuatsu* or *kuappo*. Used mainly on the battlefield, some felt it to be worse than the injury. Now it was Kwan Li's only hope.

To relieve the pressure on the brain caused by the head injury, Shin Po needed to create pressure in another part of the skull. He looked around; the ledge was not generous and gave him little scope for the violent blow needed to set up the counteraction. But Kwan Li was alive, and alive he must stay.

Perhaps it was the light or the sudden presence of another person, but Kwan Li opened his eyes wide and seemed about to speak.

"Don't thank me," said Shin Po. "If I had any sense, I'd let you rot." Then Shin Po was ready, but in a moment of clarity, Kwan Li said, "Kill me."

Shin Po couldn't believe what he heard. He'd set everything going inside him to keep this man alive. It was all he'd thought about during the long, arduous descent into the darkness. His sole purpose was to save his enemy's life, and now with success in his hand, he was being asked to relinquish it. Trust Kwan Li to be difficult; even at the threshold of death he was one person who could make Shin Po want to kill, and he could have killed Kwan Li instantly just for his contrariness.

"If you came to help me, the best thing you can do is to kill me. Even if your pressure blow works, I shall be only half alive, and that is no way for a man like me to spend the rest of his days. I am better off dead".

Shin Po was stunned, as if he had been split in half; part of him wanted Kwan Li dead—and he'd come to fight against it; another part wanted to bring Kwan Li up alive—also why he had come.

Shin Po knew, too, that if the roles were reversed, he would want only life or death, nothing in between. To save Kwan Li now would be to impose upon him a cruel life sentence, worse than any death.

"Kill me, kill . . . " urged Kwan Li's voice again, his clarity fading.

Shin Po looked at this once fine figure of a man. What would it merit him to say that this was once his enemy? Keep the enemy high, make him a worthy opponent—that was the creed he had always lived by.

Suddenly, Shin Po knew what he must do. And he must be swift. With no further thought, he struck the sharp, fatal blow that would end Kwan Li's life.

Shin Po fixed him into the sling and tugged on the rope that would haul him up. He no longer cared what the villagers thought. He had done what was right, as he saw it. He would give his old enemy a funeral befitting a warrior.

It was a little while before the rope came back down for Shin Po. When it did, he left the torch on the ledge as a memorial light to his enemy.

When he reached the top, the villagers were nodding and muttering. The same old man was waiting and was the first to speak: "You did well."

"I said I would bring him up alive or die in the attempt," reminded Shin Po.

"And you did. You did."

"Your jest is ill-timed."

"What you feared would happen did indeed happen."

"That I failed and brought him up dead?"

"No, that you succeeded and brought him up alive."

"What do you mean?" But without waiting for an answer, Shin Po strode across to where the body of

Kwan Li lay and looked down on the definitely lifeless form.

He came back and glowered at the old man, who explained, "Sometimes when we very much want something to happen, we set up a chain of events which, even if we want to change or reverse them, we can't. The wheels are set in motion in a certain direction and refuse to change. You had set up a chain of tempered steel that could not be broken; it had gone too far. You were prepared to deliver a violent healing blow. You still did—for a moment."

"Explain," said Shin Po, curtly.

"Kwan Li told us what happened. Then he died."

"But he couldn't have survived that blow. It never fails," said Shin Po, almost to himself.

"And it still won't fail when used in combat. Sometimes it takes the body a little longer to realize what the mind already knows."

"Nonsense. If that was the case, I would have been killed in combat long ago."

"When you fight, you don't think, you act—spontaneously. You don't think about what you are going to do; you do it, mind and body together. But here, you were doing a lot of thinking. By placing his death in your hands, Kwan Li gave you a greater responsibility than the one you had imposed upon yourself. You couldn't kill him, yet you couldn't let him live."

"Awkward to the last," thought Shin Po, who wasn't sure whether he had failed or succeeded. But it no longer mattered. Both men had got what they wanted, and for the only time in their lives, it was the same thing—Kwan Li's death.

"Did you meet anything in the chasm?" asked the old man.

Shin Po wasn't sure about that either. "I didn't get to the bottom of it, if that's what you mean."

"Man and the chasm are part of the mystery that is the universe, and the chasm, like man, is deep and difficult to get to the bottom of. But for as long as it's there, someone will want to try."

Shin Po went to the edge of the great craggy teeth to take a last look. The torch was steadily burning a long way down. He watched it reduce in size to a mere pinprick and slowly die. The light of Kwan Li had finally burnt out.

• • •

Where was Shin Po now? Wasn't he exactly where he would have been had he done nothing? Kwan Li would have died anyway. But Shin Po knew it was not the same, because he *had* done something.

> Same position on the circle of action,
> only now the circle was complete,
> at the return instead of the outset.
> Like going so far out into the world,
> you find yourself coming back.

Look Out—If You
Want to Get a Look In

An artist sat looking out through the *shoji* (sliding doors) across the meditation garden to the bamboo forest beyond. What, he wondered, was beyond the forest, far, far beyond, and beyond that, even farther. His mind was wandering. He must pull it back. He should have been concentrating on the inflow and outflow of his breath in preparation for ink brush drawing.

He was aware of the cool breath through his nostrils, and the warm breath at the back of his throat during the exhalation. He tried to feel its effect on his body. If he could feel the breath suffusing his body, the brush could express it with simple, flowing ease. But his mind would not stay one-pointed. It went winging off to distant lands, distant forms and expressions of painting, different materials, and even different physical approaches to holding the brush or sitting in front of his work.

Mentally, he brought together all the ways of which he had heard. When he put brush to paper, it would be in the new styles to which his world had been exposed.

He brought all the ways together in a single painting, and it was good. His body was still, but his emotions were

excited. His mind raced until a whole gallery of his work appeared before him. He looked closely and saw clearly. Underlying each painting was his own traditional way. He had adapted, not changed, the traditional. It was there, clearer, sharper, and fresher in its new setting.

His *sumi-e* tradition was in each painting, like the distilled essence of a dewdrop. He inhaled its purity and let its morning freshness permeate his being.

He felt like a mountain, a tree, a tumbling stream—strong and firm, deep-rooted and flowing, breaking around and over all obstacles.

He raised his eyes and, feeling the harmony of nature, took up his ink stick in preparation.

When the brush touched the paper—an extension of eye and hand—it painted the original Zen, regenerated with a living quality he had never known before.

• • •

He had journeyed to the distant corners of himself and found the root in its home ground, as part of everything that is or that could ever be.

Through the Garden

Upon the birth of his daughter, the emperor of a tiny kingdom summoned the court astrologers and set them to charting her future from the exact moment she came into the world.

When they had completed their task, it was with sadness that they told the emperor his daughter would meet her death at a young age by drowning—after nursing her husband through an affliction that would eventually kill him.

Grief-stricken by such terrible news, the emperor vowed she would never marry. To protect his daughter and to ensure that she saw no man, thereby having no cause to pine, he confined her to a heavily guarded room.

On rare occasions, she walked with her father in the garden, lingering longest at the peaceful corner that was the meditation garden. But her father was a busy man, and though she had her formal tuition, her brush drawing, and her music, her life was a solitary one. Her chief solace was looking upon the world from her window.

She grew to love the garden below and knew every corner of it: in spring—cherry blossoms; in winter—

snowladen pines; by moonlight—smooth stone on rippled sand in the garden of meditation, the curve of bamboo swaying in the breeze towards the dwarf trees. She watched rain showers heighten the brilliance of naturally colored stones, specially chosen and placed by the delicate sensitivity of some unseen hand and eye. A single leaf was a thing of beauty in its simplicity. Oranges and persimmons stained the green with splashes of orange. Everything had something to say to her—so much peace, so much harmony. And she came to love not only the garden, but the one who tended it. Although she never saw him, she knew that he was there—somewhere.

She wondered what the gardener looked like, and she tried to imagine him. He must be a very kind man for she knew he must love the garden in order to make it grow so well. And, as she thought about it, some of his love and attention fell upon her. It was warm, and made the windows so much wider.

Then, one day the emperor fell sick. He loved his daughter and wanted to spend as much time with her as he could. After all, he was not young any more. So she came to him for a few hours every day. Perhaps, he thought, if he had the strength to reach the *onzen*—the spa waters— would help him. He called for his entourage and, together with his daughter and her attendants, they went to the hot springs.

At the springs, there were many pools of sulphur, all steaming and bubbling at varying degrees. Finding a pool at the right temperature, the princess splashed and relaxed happily, relishing the openness of a high, blue sky and the distant horizon.

But alas, unaccustomed to so much sulphur and heat, she was overcome with exhaustion and fainted. Before she could be reached and pulled out, she drowned.

The emperor grieved bitterly for his daughter. "Why, oh, why?" he asked his advisors, "after all my precautions?"

But all the astrologers could say was: "Sire, all these years you have kept your daughter closer to you than any husband would have done, and it is written—"

The emperor raised his hand. "Yes, yes," he cried, and he prepared to die, according to the prophecy. But he didn't die—not then.

He took a walk through the gardens that he knew his daughter had loved so well, and to keep them in good order in her memory, he summoned the gardener to give him careful instructions. But the gardener could not be found.

He was eventually discovered, dead, in the tiny pool into which the princess had so often looked when she came from the garden of meditation with her father.

"He must have tripped and fallen," said an attendant. "That lame leg of his had been getting steadily worse."

"He would never have given up, though," said another. "He loved the garden and said it gave him healing, and made his pain easier to bear. Sometimes I think the garden nursed and tended *him*, not the other way round. He had a real communication with that garden and wouldn't have wanted to die anywhere else."

•   •   •

> When the emperor heard the news,
> He said nothing.
> Ripples in the sand,
> Ripples in the pool,
> And the emperor looked deep,
> And wondered.

The Living Island

Kikuchi was a great traveler. He wandered to the farthest corners of the land, and sometimes crossed the inland seas that surrounded his home of many islands. Still, he wished to find the Land of Great Age, where people lived long and did not grow old. One day, he decided to sail south in his quest.

He had not journeyed many days when a fierce storm arose. The waves crashed and thundered as if to beat his tiny vessel from the sea.

Kikuchi knew that this area was renowned for its typhoons—thought to be the place where they started—but he would not turn back. It was not his nature to retreat. Besides, the storm could abate. But it did not—it grew worse.

His boat was well constructed, but the sea tossed it around as if it were already driftwood. No longer could Kikuchi sail against what, his fears now admitted, was a typhoon.

Relentless wind, rain, and waves finally drove the boat aground. It struck with such force that Kikuchi was thrown out onto the rocks. Unconscious, he lay in a waterlogged hollow.

The following morning, Kikuchi's eyes snapped open—to see a clear sky and a high forehead of sun peering over a calm horizon. The water was like silk. After the battle of the previous night, such peace was balm to his soul. He watched the rest of the sun's face lift itself swiftly from the sea. Strangely, he did not feel cold.

He sat up and looked around him. The rocks upon which he had been thrown were off the edge of an island. The typhoon had driven great boulders inland, which had built up the shoreline. To Kikuchi, this was a definite advantage. With no boat and feeling too weak to swim far, he was, at least, able to wade ashore.

The island was remarkably warm, he found, suggesting inner heat, which meant that the island was young and not long risen from the sea—young, that is, as far as islands go, for many that arose disappeared again before they had time to cool and support life.

In his eagerness to explore, Kikuchi forgot his aching limbs. The island was bigger than he had first thought. Hollows and warm mounds of rock, some still steaming, made walking difficult.

The dark open mouths of caves begged exploration. Some smelt of sulphur, some were overwhelmingly steamy, yet others were comfortable. In one of these Kikuchi was surprised to find the rudiments of living. Until that moment, he had assumed he was alone, having seen no one.

The next yawning gap in the rock did not go far back, but it seemed to due to a deceptive collection of rock formations randomly thrown together. As Kikuchi wormed his way through the spaces between the rocks, he thought he heard a voice. Tired, he assumed it to be in his head. But his curiosity was great, and he continued searching.

The island here was a mixture of old and young. Where the sulphur was old, he could see the earth around it steaming in bubbles through thin putty.

Suddenly Kikuchi came to a fresh rock movement, where the putty-like surface had given way. Here, he found the owner of the voice. The man was not scalded or burned, but he was trapped. Kikuchi could see he had to be careful how he moved as he could make things worse. For the balance of rock was delicate.

"Hold on," he called to the trapped man. "I must move slowly."

"I don't know where you came from, but I'm very glad you are here," said the man. "The island still moves."

"Are you alone?" asked Kikuchi, working and talking at the same time.

"No," said the trapped man.

"I saw no one else."

"The island is big, but when I do not return, my friend will come looking."

"Do you have a boat?" asked Kikuchi.

"We were sick and the current brought us here, but the boat was damaged. We have been trying to repair it."

Kikuchi worked as quickly and carefully as he could. He was soon exhausted, but he pushed himself on. Then a tremor from the island buckled their surroundings. And it seemed to be getting hotter.

In his tiredness, Kikuchi did not move fast enough, and suddenly he, too, was trapped. Their only hope was now the third man, and the continued vibration meant help had to come soon.

They hoped he was already looking for them. The island was fermenting. They were living on the edge of the earth's eruption.

Then there was another rock disturbance—this time a human hand was the cause. Scrambling into view was the third man, who called out,

"Are you there?"

"Yes, yes," came the eager reply of the first trapped man.

"There is just time to get you out."

"What kept you?" asked the man's friend.

"I wanted to test the boat; but there was so little time."

"And is the boat safe?"

"I don't know. But if we are lucky, we will live to find out."

At last, the third man broke through the rocks—and stopped.

"Yes, there are two of us," said his friend, quietly.

Kikuchi resigned himself to his fate. He knew there was only time for one of them to be freed; otherwise they all might die.

In the momentary hesitation, Kikuchi saw the love and the pain in the rescuer's eyes as he looked first at his friend, and then at himself, a stranger.

Then, to the astonishment of both trapped men, the rescuer went straight to Kikuchi. He worked feverishly, tearing at the rocks as if his own life depended upon it. Kikuchi knew his rescuer loved his friend, so why was he doing this? He, himself, was nothing to the man.

Silently, the rescuer worked, clawing like a demon, yet instinctively knowing what to attack first. Surely only a great force could drive a man thus, and Kikuchi felt it was love, yet they were strangers.

When he was at last free, Kikuchi flexed his limbs and worked as best he could alongside his benefactor to free the other trapped man. The whole island felt as if, at any moment, it would be blasted from the sea or overwhelmed by it.

With little help from Nature, all three men were finally free and racing to the shore. Once they were in the boat, fleeing the wrath of the sea bed and hoping to escape any cross currents or giant waves, Kikuchi could no longer contain himself; he had to know.

"Why did you dig me out before your friend, whom I know you love well?"

There was no immediate reply. Then their rescuer said, "In so short a time, only my friend's life had the force to drive me through your rescue to his. Had I gone to him first, you could still be there."

Kikuchi understood. He knew he had been merely the surface that had to be attacked with enough force to reach the target beyond.

They looked back at the exploding island and saw, not destruction in the upheaval, but rebirth—new land emerging from old foundations. And Kikuchi felt all the layers within himself that he had ever been, spanning many lifetimes. He was earth, with all its upheavals, wrought in fire; he was change, blown and buffeted by the wind; and he was the calm, rocking gently on silken water. He was ready to continue his quest.

Joan Baxter has been a student of Eastern philosophy, martial arts, various forms of yoga, and zen. She teaches yoga, self-defense and relaxation to women and older members of the community. During her life, she has practiced aikido and attained the grade of shodan black belt in karate.

Currently, she is a member of the Guild of Professional Massage Practitioners in England and works with aromatherapy at a natural health clinic. She participates in the Brahma Kumaris World Spiritual University and wrote these teaching stories as a result of her many travels and meetings with spiritual teachers in Asia and the Orient.